Presented to:

Date:

From:

Volume 1
Training for
Spiritual
Excellence

Daily
Strength
for the
Battle ©

You,
God's Word,
5 minutes

By Scott McChrystal

Daily Strength for the Battle: Training for Spiritual Excellence
By Scott McChrystal

Published by Warrior Spirit Publications.

Contact information:
Web site: *www.dailystrengthforthebattle.com*
E-mail: *contact@dailystrengthforthebattle.com*
Mail: *Warrior Spirit Publications*
       P.O. Box 8125, Springfield, MO 65801

Design by Marc McBride

ISBN: 978-0-615-31539-3

Printed in the United States of America

To my Dad, MG Herbert J. McChrystal, Jr., USA (Ret) whose life inspired me to join the military and whose personal example set the standard for selfless service as member of the Profession of Arms.

To my loving wife of 36 years, Judy, for her love, support, and encouragement to serve the Lord with all my heart.

To all military veterans, past and present, and their families who have served God and Country so nobly and selflessly. Only the Lord and those who have walked that path can fully grasp the incredible commitment, dedication, and sacrifices you have made. Thank you. The prayers and support of our nation are with you.

Contents

Contents

Caring for Others:
The Buck Stops Here 88

"Scott McChrystal knows God and he knows military personnel. Strength for the Battle *brings the two together in a powerful way. Scott's 30 plus years of military leadership enables him to speak with biblical authority into the minds of veterans. This is an excellent tool for bringing veterans into the transformational presence of God.*"

— George O. Wood, General Superintendent,
Assemblies of God General Council

"The stresses of military training and combat heighten spiritual awareness. Scott McChrystal's book hits that mark beautifully! These stories and devotions are solidly focused on God's Word, and written in a way that uniquely connect with the military. The Lord prepared him for this work: first as an infantry platoon leader in Vietnam, a master parachutist and Ranger; then as an Army chaplain serving soldiers and families across the Army; he is father of two soldiers."

— Kenneth L. Farmer, Jr., M.D., MG, USA (Ret)

"Daily Strength for the Battle *is a daily devotional that combines spiritual wisdom and practical insights in a readily accessible manner that is sure to appeal to persons both in and outside of the military environment. I highly recommend this new book.*"

— Rich Hammar, church law authority, writer, speaker

"Chaplain Scott McChrystal is a combat veteran and spiritual warrior who has captured the essence of winning the daily fight against mankind's spiritual enemy. This is a good field manual for every Christian who wants to be prepared for battle"

— LTG Jerry Boykin, USA (RET), former Commander of
Delta Force and Commander of USASOC

"*Chaplain Scott McChrystal served as one of the most beloved chaplains ever at the U.S. Military Academy at West Point and throughout the Army. A former infantry officer and Vietnam veteran, Chaplain McChrystal's overall military service have enabled him to touch thousands of America's magnificent warriors. He will influence many more through this powerful devotional book.*"

— *Dave Roever, decorated Vietnam veteran, Military speaker*

"*Every man, particularly a warrior, needs time every day with his King. Focused, purposeful, gripping time. And if he's a busy man (know any warrior who's not?), the punch of that time is served well by a directed devotional book like this one offered by my friend, Scott McChrystal, who is himself a tested warrior. And a busy, focused, and purposeful man. Enjoy the journey with him. Drive on!*"

— *Stu Weber, Former Special Forces Officer and Vietnam veteran, author, speaker, pastor*

"*Given the multitude of challenges faced by our nation's service members, Chaplain Scott McChrystal's* Daily Strength for the Battle *is a powerful devotional tool for military men, women, and families. This inspirational guide, drawn from Chaplain McChrystal's significant experience as an infantry leader and a chaplain spiritual leader, is a very practical means by which we might all 'put on the armor of God' on a daily basis. I truly applaud this powerful spiritual ammunition to promote 'Faith in the Foxhole and Hope on the Home Front' for military men and women around the globe.*"

— *Major General Bob Dees, US Army (Ret), Executive Director, CCCI Military Ministry*

Introduction

People come from all different backgrounds. I come from a military background and consider it a great privilege to have been associated with the military community for 35 years. I can never repay the debt I owe the military for the opportunity it afforded me to serve as a member of the profession of arms.

My years of service with the United States Army (31 years active duty) ended in 2005, but I hope my most significant contributions to this community lie ahead. I want to contribute to the spiritual life and vitality of service members and their families who serve our Armed Forces so courageously and selflessly. Included with this group are the multiplied millions who are military veterans and their families.

The term *veteran* actually encompasses all military folks, past and present. Perhaps the best definition of a veteran I've ever seen comes from an anonymous source:

> A "veteran" — whether active duty, discharged, retired or reserve — is someone who, at one point in his life, wrote a blank check made payable to the "United States of America," for an amount "up to and including his/her life."

The public at large doesn't understand the hardships and sacrifices unique to the military community. I'm not sure they ever will. This is not a criticism, but an observation worth consideration as America tries to support the community of warriors who keep our nation free.

As my act of support, I offer this devotional book because I firmly believe that hope for the military community — past and present — rests in a relationship with the living God through His Son Jesus Christ.

This little book is the first in a series of manuals for Christian growth, written with content that is biblically based and carefully applied to life within the military community. The attempt has been to make these messages brief, practical and relevant.

The first volume, *Strength for the Battle: Training for Spiritual Excellence*, rests on the conviction that growth in the Christian life does not happen by accident, but rather by diligence and effort in seeking God. Military people understand commitment and hard work. They also comprehend words like *training* and *excellence*. The Bible provides indisputable evidence that applying oneself to growing in Christ will produce positive results.

I trust that you will find encouragement, strength, wisdom and motivation toward excellence in your Christian walk as you read this book. ■

Christian growth and maturity take effort on a consistent basis. With consistency noted as a key principle, this book is most useful when read on a daily basis. Reading time should take about five minutes.

Each volume of *Daily Strength for the Battle*:

- Contains seven weeks of devotions, with one devotion per day

- Each week relates to one theme

- Each weekly theme begins with a practical illustration designed to demonstrate the relevance and importance of each theme

- All daily devotions incorporate topics related to the weekly theme

- All daily devotions begin with a Bible verse related to the topic

A suggested way to approach your devotional time could include the following:

- Prayer — ask the Lord to open your heart and mind to the truth of His Word.

- Read the verse at the beginning of the devotional and then paraphrase it in your own words

- Read the devotional

- Try to answer the following questions:

- What biblical truth does this devotional talk about?

- How is the truth applied in the devotional?

- Do I believe this truth could be important for my own life?

- How can I apply this truth to my own life?

- Close in prayer: ask God to help you integrate this truth into your own life.

Five minutes a day may not seem like much, but you can experience wonderful growth in your Christian life and walk by consistently having these short devotions. The Lord will honor your efforts to honor Him.

What God Says

At the back of this book, I've included a section called "What God Says" (pages 100–129). It contains a list of issues and topics that most people just assume they understand. But in His Word, the Bible, God has addressed each of these issues of life in a way that is both clear and relevant to your life. The verses listed under each topic are just a start, but if you want to know more, the Bible contains many other verses related to these topics. ■

Overcoming the Giants in Your Life

The Philistine said, "This day I defy the ranks of Israel! Give me a man and let us fight each other." On hearing the Philistine's words, Saul and all the Israelites were dismayed and terrified.
(1 Samuel 17:10,11)

Trials are as old as humanity. They are part of life, and all of us will face them. Some trials are giants. While there are many questions we could ask about life's difficult seasons, the most relevant question is this: When trials come, how will I respond?

The verses cited above refer to a time in ancient Israel when a giant named Goliath single-handedly defied the armies of Israel and the God they served.

How did Israel respond? The Bible tells us that King Saul and the Israelite army were dismayed and terrified. Fortunately for Israel, one man had a different response. His name was David.

David didn't run from this trial. He stood and embraced it. He sought the Lord's help as he challenged the 9-foot giant in a fight to the death. With God's help, David prevailed and won a tremendous victory for Saul and the nation of Israel.

David did several things that worked together to give him victory. But nothing was more crucial than placing his trust in the Lord. Consider his words spoken to Goliath immediately before the fight:

> *You come against me with sword and spear and javelin, but I come against you in the name of the L*ORD *Almighty, the God of the armies of Israel, whom you have defied. This day the L*ORD *will hand you over to me, and I'll strike you down and cut off your head.*
> *(1 Samuel 17:45,46)*

When trials come, and they surely will, place your trust in the Lord to help you.

In the early 1980s my family and I traveled to Alton, Mo., to preach at a Palm Sunday morning service. Following church, we were invited to have lunch with a Vietnam veteran, a Marine. I don't recall his name, but I'll never forget him or the dinner we had with them that day.

This Marine had faced many trials in his life, but his response to one particular challenge has impacted me until this day. You see, this Marine has lost both legs in combat. He had only stumps, so short that prostheses were out of the question. At church I had seen him in a wheelchair. When we drove to his home following church, we saw something quite different.

As we arrived at his home, his wife greeted us warmly. About five minutes later the Marine appeared, his body and clothes wet with perspiration. We quickly learned why. He had just climbed down from the roof of his house where he had been putting finishing touches on the new roof he had installed during the previous week. Yes, he had shingled his entire roof by himself! This man without legs was hardly a disabled veteran.

He quickly excused himself to get cleaned up. Looking like an Olympic gymnast, he shot up the stairs on his hands. His heavily muscled arms propelled him up the stairs as easily as most normal people climb stairs with their legs.

Over dinner, this veteran exuded thanksgiving to God for his life, never once mentioning a word about the loss of his legs. He faced this trial with faith and courage. Through God's strength, he was a champion.

Let David's example and the example of this brave Marine encourage you to face your trials squarely by turning to God for strength. You can trust Him with your cares. God helped David conquer a giant. He helped a veteran Marine gain victory over his wounds. He will surely help you. ■

Knowing Our Limits

No temptation has seized you except what is common to man. And God is faithful; he will not let you be tempted beyond what you can bear. But when you are tempted, he will also provide a way out so that you can stand up under it.
(1 Corinthians 10:13)

Effective leaders have the knack for challenging soldiers to the limit without breaking their spirit. Even before the outcome has occurred, they somehow know that the experience will be beneficial — for individual soldiers and for the unit.

In the midst of the trial it is easy to doubt the outcome. It helps when soldiers can trust that their leaders know what they are doing.

Life has its trials. This verse assures us that God is a leader who knows what He is doing. He knows your strengths. He knows your weaknesses. He knows your limits. He'll never overextend you. He will provide a way for you to make it!

But that's not all. He uses trials to grow you physically, mentally, and spiritually.

Bottom line: God knows your full potential and He wants to take you to the very limits. ■

Hanging Tough

Dear friends, do not be surprised at the painful trial you are suffering, as though something strange were happening to you. But rejoice that you participate in the sufferings of Christ, so that you may be overjoyed when his glory is revealed.
(1 Peter 4:12,13, NIV)

War is tough, uncompromising and unforgiving. And yet, American combat veterans who have fought and suffered for this nation will almost always tell you that the causes of freedom and justice were worth whatever hardships they experienced. They know that freedom isn't free, but it's worth the price.

Spiritual warfare involves suffering as well. Here the apostle Peter is providing encouragement to early Christians going through tough trials. Some were probably on the verge of giving up. Peter's message was a call to hang tough. He assured them that God would make it all worthwhile in the end.

Tough times exist today as well. Are you going through tough trials in your Christian walk? You may even be tempted to give up. But God says, "Hang in there, soldier! Don't give up! You will be richly rewarded for your faithfulness." ■

Counting the Cost

Anyone who does not take his cross and follow me
is not worthy of me.
(Matthew 10:38)

Basic training is not an easy time, nor is it intended to be. Every class has those individuals who start but do not finish.

The reasons can be varied, but a frequent one is the failure to count the cost. The military is a demanding business, and only those who have counted the cost will make it.

The Christian life is no easy road either. Jesus didn't mince words.

His reference to "take his cross" simply means that the Christian life includes hardship in following God's will. Jesus not only carried His cross. He died on it.

If you have made the decision to carry your cross and follow Christ, congratulations! But don't expect that it will be easy.

But be sure of this. The decision to follow Christ is the most important choice any person can ever make. Won't you choose to follow Him today? ■

Avoiding Sin

In the spring, at the time when kings go off to war, David sent Joab out with the king's men and the whole Israelite army. They destroyed the Ammonites and besieged Rabbah. But David remained in Jerusalem.
(2 Samuel 11:1)

Surrendering to the temptation of sin cost King David dearly. When you read the rest of 2 Samuel 11, you discover he not only committed adultery with Bathsheba, but even tried to conceal his sin by ordering the death of her innocent husband, Uriah.

Could David have avoided this sin? An AAR (After-Action Review) of this episode yields a valuable clue in the phrase "at the time when kings go off to war." Although it cannot be proven, it seems fair to suppose that David would not have committed this sin had he been with his army. "But David remained in Jerusalem."

Two applications seem evident here. First, avoiding the disasters of sin often begins by consciously staying away from situations that tempt us to do the wrong thing. Secondly, giving serious thought to the adverse consequences of sin can dissuade us from committing the wrong act.

Sin can be avoided. Everyone wins. ■

Carry Your Cross

Endure hardship with us like a good soldier
of Christ Jesus.
(2 Timothy 2:3)

It is common knowledge that hardship is a part of military life. In fact, effective preparation for combat requires training that closely approximates the conditions of real conflict. Cheap substitutes for tough, realistic training don't work.

In this verse the old veteran, Paul, is telling the young soldier, Timothy, that the Christian life is not for patsies. It requires guts and determination to endure the hardships that are certain to come.

Paul had every right to make this challenge due to the incredible suffering he had experienced for the cause of Christ. He had endured shipwrecks, lashing with whips, beatings with rods, imprisonment, and even stoning. Paul's body bore the marks of his service for Jesus Christ.

Want to be a good soldier for the Lord? Be willing to endure the hardships that are part of the Christian walk. This doesn't mean that you go looking for hardships. But when they come into your life as you try to serve God, don't run from them. Drive on!

Jesus endured the cross for you. Be willing to carry your cross for Him. ∎

Tough Demands

But after his disciples had gathered around him, he got up and went back into the city. The next day he and Barnabas left for Derbe.
(Acts 14:20)

Perseverance is an essential quality for success in the military. The mission often demands that we keep going no matter what. Victory rarely goes to the fainthearted.

The Christian life can make tough demands, too. This verse tells us about the perseverance of the apostle Paul. He had just been stoned and left for dead outside the city of Lystra.

Did Paul give up? No way! After the disciples prayed for him, he got back up and went right back to face the crowd that had stoned him.

The Bible contains the stories of many other men and women of faith who stood their ground in the face of adversity. And there are many people still alive today who have overcome extreme challenges. You undoubtedly know men and women like this.

Are you facing a battle and feeling like giving up? Don't! Your struggle is nothing you and God can't handle. Be an overcomer.

Stay in the fight. Victory will come. ∎

Facing Your Battles

> *Have I not commanded you? Be strong and*
> *courageous. Do not be terrified; do not be*
> *discouraged, for the LORD your God will be*
> *with you wherever you go.*
> *(Joshua 1:9)*

After Moses died, God appointed Joshua to lead the people of Israel through many battles before they could fully claim the land God had promised.

For over two decades, Joshua and the Israelites remained at war with neighboring tribes and nations. In a few battles, they tasted defeat and discouragement. But they never gave up. With the Lord's help, Joshua and the people of Israel prevailed.

Some people today seem to miss two important truths. First, in this life we will face numerous battles we cannot win in our own strength. These battles go beyond the physical battlefield. They include personal struggles in areas like self-worth, communication in marriage, finances, and relationships with children.

Second, God's presence is not limited to the pages of the Old Testament. He stands ready today to help you with the battles you face — even today.

Your life can be one of victory. Are you allowing the Lord to help you win the battles you face? ∎

Crossroads Experiences

The heart of the discerning acquires knowledge;
the ears of the wise seek it out.
(Proverbs 18:15)

God's knowledge and wisdom are available for those who genuinely want to listen and learn. His Holy Spirit can speak to any person who will keep an open heart and mind to truth, even someone who does not really know Him in a personal way. I say this with confidence because it happened to me at a most crucial time in my life.

In South Vietnam in early 1972, I was serving in the northernmost U.S. military sector, known as I Corps. I was an Infantry platoon leader in an infantry battalion whose mission was to interdict the enemy's progress southward in the rest of South Vietnam. It was a tough mission for many reasons — booby traps and changing rules of engagement were two of the most frustrating. Rules of engagement governed the ability of U.S. forces to use force against the enemy, and these rules were especially challenging around built-up areas with a largely civilian population.

This particular day my platoon was to fly by helicopter into an unsecured area, set up a patrol base, and send out squad-sized patrols in search of the enemy. My greatest initial concern focused on enemy dispositions near the proposed area of insertion. The enemy often lurked in concealed positions to ambush incoming aircraft. Another tactic was to saturate landing zones with booby traps. Sometimes these tactics were used in combination.

A potentially complicating factor for this mission was the presence of a village about a thousand meters from the scheduled landing area. We normally used preparatory fires on the objective area prior to landing. Any civilians nearby would be in serious danger.

We crowded my platoon onto four UH1H helicopters, each armed with M-60 machine guns at the left and right side doors. Accompanying our flight were two Cobra helicopter gunships and one C & C (command and control) helicopter that carried leaders who were directing the airmobile insertion.

Once in the air, I monitored the battalion command radio net, the frequency the battalion operations officer (known as the S3) was using to communicate with all pilots and with the battalion commander back at the battalion firebase. The S3 passed the word that we were five minutes from the objective area. At that point I could feel the butterflies begin in the pit of my stomach.

I mentally rehearsed actions on the objective as we prepared to land and secure the area.

Suddenly the S3 came over the radio and ordered the lead helicopter to pull back from the objective and continue in a wider orbit until further notice. He had spotted several personnel on the landing zone, apparently dressed in black and possibly carrying weapons. I continued to listen to the S3 as he discussed the situation with the Cobra pilots and with the commander back at the firebase. Finally, he gave orders to the Cobra pilots to place fire on the objective area. Immediately, I saw the Cobras make a sharp turn and begin their descent to the target area. In just a few seconds, the landing zone would be enveloped in a hailstorm of bullets and rockets. Any person caught in their sights would almost certainly die.

The Cobra pilots did their duty with deadly accuracy. The helicopters carrying my platoon were cleared to land. As we hovered to within a couple feet of the ground, I jumped off into a windstorm of dust created by the powerful rotor blades and ran out away from the chopper.

With my platoon on the ground, the choppers quickly left the landing zone. I checked to make sure each squad was performing measures to secure the area. We posted 360-degree security at sufficient distances to protect us from ambush while simultaneously sweeping the immediate area for booby traps. None were found.

Our attention now focused on attending to five personnel present in the landing zone when the Cobras made their firing run. Not a pretty sight. I will spare you the details except to say that two of the people were still alive — barely. All five appeared to be between the ages of 5 and 16. They were wearing what looked like black pajamas and had been carrying sticks. Perhaps they had been searching for firewood. I don't know. As I surveyed the carnage, I recall saying out loud, "This never should have happened."

I immediately directed my RTO (radio/telephone operator) to call the pilots who had just dropped us off. We needed their assistance with transporting the three killed and two wounded boys to the rear area. Maybe emergency medical help could save at least one of the survivors. Within three to four minutes, the choppers were back. We loaded the five personnel and they were in the air in minutes, but I doubt the two survived.

About 15 minutes later, another helicopter landed and the battalion command sergeant major motioned to me to get on the aircraft. Apparently, the battalion commander wanted to see me back at the battalion firebase.

The helicopter landed and I was escorted to the commander's office. He pointed me toward a seat then looked at me for a few seconds before speaking. I sensed he was choosing his words very carefully.

"Lieutenant," he began, "I know you didn't like what just happened on the objective. I didn't either. I understood that you spoke aloud within the hearing of some of your men that the incident never should have happened. We need to talk about this."

Unknown to me, the battalion sergeant major had apparently landed on our objective shortly after my platoon had landed and overheard my comment about the incident.

From my perspective as a young officer, I did view the event as clearly avoidable. It appeared to me that young civilians had died needlessly. I was very angry, and the commander knew it.

My battalion commander, a veteran of multiple tours in Vietnam, had a different perspective. He explained that he had seen American soldiers wounded or killed when the enemy used civilians as decoys. He furthered explained that the village had been properly warned about impending U.S. operations and that the area was a free-fire zone strictly off limits to all villagers.

He continued, "I don't like to see any innocent people hurt or killed, but my first responsibility is to protect soldiers under my command. You and your platoon could have been victims of the enemy's deceptive tactics. I was not willing to take that chance. I gave the order for the Cobra pilots to place fire on the objective area."

Like a father, he followed with this: "Scott, war can be very tough. I want to offer you a choice. You have already completed more combat field duty than normally required for lieutenants in this battalion. I will be happy to reassign you to a rear area job. If you don't want that and would rather return to your platoon, I need your word that you will not second-guess my decisions in front of your platoon again. Is that clear?"

Have you ever had one of those moments when you know that what is about to happen could change the course of your life? I call these "crossroads experiences," and I was definitely having one.

If ever I needed wisdom, I needed it then. From seemingly out of nowhere, it came. It was the Lord speaking to my heart, but I didn't realize it back then. I was not a Christian, and I knew almost nothing about the things of God. The voice, though not audible, spoke and told me to listen to my commander. That he was a man of reason and experience. He clearly hated that civilians had been hurt, but he was correct to take actions he deemed necessary to protect his troops. I sensed that I should tell the commander that I wanted to get back to my platoon, that I would not second-guess my commander's decisions in front of my men again.

I followed that counsel to the letter. I shook hands with the commander, saluted, and left his office. I got on a chopper and returned to my platoon.

Decades have passed, but I've never forgotten that day. The faces of those Vietnamese kids haunt my memory. But the Lord has given me perspective. I am convinced he made what he believed was the right decision for that place and that time. On top of that, I can see that the Lord used him to teach me some tough lessons about war and the need for leaders to maintain discipline and self-control at all times.

Over the years since I put my faith in Christ in 1973, I have seen the Lord intervene countless times in my life. I also know that many times He was acting behind the scenes even when I didn't know it. That day in Vietnam was just one example.

Do you need wisdom and guidance? Ask the Lord. He will guide you. You can count on it. ■

Are You Listening?

The Lord came and stood there, calling as at the other times, "Samuel! Samuel!" Then Samuel said, "Speak, for your servant is listening."
(1 Samuel 3:10)

Communication is critical on the battlefield. Commanders cannot control the fight unless they can communicate with their units. Yet the nature of communication demands a two-way effort. Leaders must communicate guidance; subordinate leaders must communicate to their leaders, but they must also listen and obey.

Samuel, though just a young boy, expressed a desire to hear from God — and the willingness to obey Him.

Some people wander aimlessly through life, not knowing if God still speaks. The truth is He does. The primary means is through His eternal Word. He speaks in other ways as well, but especially through prayer.

Other people express their concerns to God in prayer, but never stick around long enough to hear the answer. Sometimes it's good to practice simply listening to God.

Our Heavenly Commander still speaks today. Even in the midst of a violent firefight or during some other crisis, the Lord will provide the guidance you need.

Are you listening?

Seeking Guidance

So David inquired of the LORD, "Shall I go and attack the Philistines? Will you hand them over to me?" The LORD answered him, "Go, for I will surely hand the Philistines over to you."
(2 Samuel 5:19)

King David was a brave soldier and proven commander in combat. Undoubtedly he went through troop-leading procedures in a thorough manner, especially prior to combat. But note this verse. David also sought guidance from the Lord.

And he is not alone. Through the centuries military leaders have continued to turn to the Lord when the stakes are high.

Our human tendency is to place too much emphasis on our knowledge, skills and experience. All of these can help, but seeking the Lord's guidance is the most important step we can take prior to entering a battle — any kind of battle.

The Lord wants us to seek his guidance in the daily challenges of life. Issues like marriage, raising children, handling finances, and setting priorities are all important in our lives. We don't have to handle them on our own.

What about you? Do you consult your Heavenly Commander prior to the combat situations in life? ■

Essential Information

Jesus went out to a mountainside to pray, and spent the night praying to God. When morning came, he called his disciples to him and chose twelve of them, whom he also designated apostles.
(Luke 6:12,13)

Military leadership includes sound and timely decision-making as one of its core principles. Having the essential information and guidance is critical to making the best decisions. Failure in this area may cause unnecessary casualties and even prevent mission accomplishment.

In our personal lives, essential information and guidance are equally necessary. Ironically, we frequently overlook our best source of help — our Heavenly Commander-in-Chief.

Jesus consulted His Father all night before choosing His 12 disciples. Jesus knew the importance of the decision facing Him. He wanted to do His Father's will.

Our tendency is to think that all essential information will come from human levels. We can get much help from these sources, but they are no substitute for information directly from the Lord.

Do you know that your decisions are important to the Lord? God will provide the essential information and guidance you need as you read His Word and pray. ■

Guidance for the Future

Blessed is the one who reads the words of this prophecy, and blessed are those who hear it and take to heart what is written in it, because the time is near.
(Revelation 1:3)

Military operations require extensive planning. A Concept Plan (CONPLAN) contains the combatant commander's strategic concept and other information deemed necessary by the combatant commander to complete planning. The plan speaks to some future time, but does not specify the exact date and time.

The Book of Revelation, in many respects, is God's CONPLAN for the future. It doesn't lay out all the details, but it does sketch the concept and information necessary for His army to be ready when the plan is actually executed.

This verse provides excellent counsel and guidance for every soldier. In essence, it says, "You will be blessed if you read and obey what this plan says. Don't fool around. The plan will become reality soon!"

So we don't have to fear the future. God has it all mapped out and under control. And in His time He will execute it.

Be ready. Follow His guidance! ∎

Listening to Advice

The way of a fool seems right to him,
but a wise man listens to advice.
(Proverbs 12:15)

Few enjoy being around a "know it all." This kind of person is usually a "legend in his own mind" — but not in anyone else's.

Soldiers notice leaders who are "know it alls." They resent those in authority over them who refuse to listen to their ideas and suggestions. While some are mature enough to overlook this kind of an attitude in a boss, others quit trying to give their best. They don't feel that extra effort will make any difference.

God is certainly clear on this issue. From this verse it is obvious that a leader acts wisely in listening to advice — from seniors, peers and even subordinates. Only the fool has all the answers.

A word of caution. If questioned, most leaders would say they are good listeners. In actuality, many don't listen as well as they think they do. Good listening takes much practice and hard work. It's just not easy.

If you have soldiers under you, what would they say about your openness to advice?

It's never too late to change! ■

Obtaining Wisdom

*King Solomon was greater in riches and wisdom
than all the other kings of the earth.*
(1 Kings 10:23)

Life can become really complex, and even more so as
the world becomes increasingly global. Take the global
war on terror, for example. It has an incredible number of
moving pieces to consider. Civic leaders, military leaders
and soldiers at all levels need wisdom in order to carry
out their tasks effectively.

How can we obtain wisdom? Training, experience,
combat intelligence, etc., are good sources. But there's a
better source. Solomon, the wisest man who ever lived,
got his wisdom from God.

Do you know how he got it? He simply asked. As a
young man who had just succeeded his father, David, to
the throne, he confessed to the Lord that he was unable
to govern properly. Solomon needed discernment and
wisdom, and the Lord granted his request.

We err badly if we think our knowledge and experience
equal the wisdom we need in a particular situation.
We can be thankful for what God has given us, but He
always has more wisdom to share.

Do you need wisdom in your life? Consider following
Solomon's example. Ask God. ∎

Choices Matter

Choose my instruction instead of silver, knowledge rather than choice gold, for wisdom is more precious than rubies, and nothing you desire can compare with her.
(Proverbs 8:10,11)

Have you stopped lately to think about the impact of choices? Some are more important than others. But be sure of this: Choices do matter.

A young man was brought by ambulance to the emergency room with severe injuries suffered in a motorcycle accident. While he was going to survive the ordeal, he would never be the same. Sadly, the young man had made the choice not to wear sufficient protective clothing.

Fighting the good fight of faith is about making the right choices. It starts with evaluating how you make choices. Are you making your choices according to your own wisdom, or do you seek the Lord's wisdom for making decisions?

The writer of these verses, King Solomon, tells us that God's wisdom is superior to anything we can desire.

Want to make smart choices? Seek wisdom from God. ∎

Doing the Harder Right

*Don't you know that when you offer yourselves to
someone to obey him as slaves, you are slaves to
the one whom you obey — whether you are slaves
to sin, which leads to death, or to obedience,
which leads to righteousness?*
(Romans 6:16)

Anyone who has served in the military understands the
importance of obedience. From the beginning of basic
training, recruits quickly learn that obedience is key to
survival. As service members progress in their training
and experience, they learn that obedience has many
advantages.

To demonstrate that obedience is vital in all services,
consider that the word "obey" appears in every version
of the oath of office that both enlisted and officers are
required to execute. The oath of enlistment into the United
States Armed Forces is administered by any commissioned
officer to any person enlisting or re-enlisting for a term of
service into any branch of the military.

The officer asks the person or persons to raise their
right hand and repeat the oath after him. In the oath are
these words: "That I will obey the orders of the President
of the United States and the orders of the officers
appointed over me."

Obedience to the Lord is vital as well. I have seen firsthand how obedience to God has paid big dividends for those serving in the military. This obedience can take many different forms, but one area involves telling the truth.

I remember the phone call from my battalion commander at Fort Bragg. One of our engineer noncommissioned officers was being brought up on charges — serious charges. When he told me the name, I could hardly believe it. The individual was Staff Sergeant Smith*, a highly respected leader in the unit. My commander asked that I meet with SSG Smith.

He reported to my office. I invited him to sit down as we began our conversation. I learned that he not only was being charged with possessing drugs, but also with acting as a drug distributor. If the charges were proven to be true, his career was history. All the hard work and great service he had done was down the drain.

From my years as an Infantry officer, I had developed a rather direct approach in matters of this sort. After listening to SSG Smith, I asked this question: "SSG Smith, are you guilty of the charges?"

* Name has been changed.

I followed that with this statement: "If you can't speak the truth to me, I can't help you. I must know the whole truth."

Without batting an eye, SSG Smith looked directly at me and answered: "Sir, I am guilty on both counts. I have made a very serious mistake and I am ashamed of my actions. I have disgraced myself, my unit and the United States Army."

An amazing thing happened. By leveling with me and telling the truth from the beginning, we were able to focus immediately on the next steps to take. The first was to talk about his relationship with the Lord. SSG Smith didn't know much about matters of faith, but he believed in God. As I shared further, he asked clarifying questions. Within a few minutes, he asked me to lead him in prayer to accept Jesus into his life. No pressure, no coercion. This soldier knew he was a sinner and wanted to make things right with God.

Next we talked about his legal situation with the Army. He had committed a serious offense, and he was going to get hammered. No question about that. Amazingly, however, because he accepted full responsibility for his actions, he saw no need for a lawyer. He would simply confess his crime and ask for mercy.

Honestly, I wasn't sure mercy would even be part of the equation as the military authorities dealt with his case. But his willingness to openly admit his wrongdoing without excuses caught the attention of his leadership chain of command. It caught my attention as well.

When SSG Smith appeared for his court-martial, he had many supporters to speak on his behalf. To a man, the leadership in the battalion was convinced that SSG Smith had learned a hard lesson. If there was any way to restore him back to active duty, they unanimously recommended that he be granted another chance.

The legal decision handed down at the Courts Martial hit him hard. Two years at the Disciplinary Barracks at Fort Leavenworth, Kansas. Following that, he would be given a dishonorable discharge from the Army. That decision didn't seem to be wrapped in mercy. And by the way, he was reduced to the rank of private.

Private Smith didn't let the decision deter him. He decided to trust God and attempt to make the most of the situation. He promised to keep me updated with periodic phone calls detailing his progress. After several weeks,

Obedience

I received the first call. To my astonishment, he sounded upbeat about his experience and indicated that the cadre at the prison seemed inclined to support him as much as possible. He voiced his strong trust in God.

It was the second phone call that got my attention. His performance as a prisoner proved to be so stellar that the Army was now reconsidering its decision to discharge him following the serving of his sentence. He asked me to pray.

As the months rolled on, the situation seemed to change to the point of being miraculous. Not only was it looking like PVT Smith would be given a chance to remain on active duty, but he was now candidating to join the elite Army Rangers.

Unfortunately, I lost communication with PVT Smith when my family and I moved to Korea. The last communication I had with him indicated that he would be resuming active duty for sure, most likely with one of the Army Ranger battalions.

Is obedience important to the Lord? It is so crucial that Jesus spoke these words: "If you love me, you will obey what I command" (John 14:15).

SSG Smith had clearly been disobedient once. But he asked the Lord for forgiveness and proved his sincerity by being obedient to the truth. SSG Smith chose the harder right over the easier wrong. He chose obedience. ■

God's Authority

*So the L*ORD *said to Solomon, "Since this is your attitude and you have not kept my covenant and my decrees, which I commanded you, I will most certainly tear the kingdom away from you and give it to one of your subordinates."*
(1 Kings 11:11)

Have you ever witnessed a capable soldier lose rank, position or even career because of disobedience? What a waste!

Examples of disobedience include soldiers of all ranks — even generals. Looking deeper into situations of this nature often reveals an attitude of rebellion toward authority. This attitude is not always noticeable on the surface, but sooner or later it comes out.

As critical as obedience to military authority is, obedience to God's authority is even more important. Solomon, the wisest man who ever lived, found this out the hard way. His rebellion and disobedience toward God cost him dearly, and many others as well.

People in the military environment generally understand and respond to authority quite well. But it is not always the case in other parts of their lives.

This begs an important question: Should God have authority in all facets of our lives? What do you think? ■

Consequences of Disobedience

*But Samuel replied: "Does the L*ORD *delight in burnt*
offerings and sacrifices as much as in obeying
*the voice of the L*ORD*? To obey is better than to*
sacrifice, and to heed is better than the fat of rams.
(1 Samuel 15:22)

Have you ever observed soldiers with great abilities
fail because they refused to submit to a leader's
authority? They simply chose to disobey.

King Saul suffered the consequences of disobedience.
God chose him from all the men of Israel to be king.
But Saul's rule ended with his life. He never had a
dynasty.

Refusing to destroy the Amalekites completely as
God had commanded through the prophet Samuel,
Saul did as he pleased for selfish gain. His rebellion
cost him his kingship, and ultimately favor with
God.

Admittedly, doing our own thing can seem very
tempting. But any time we choose to disobey what we
know God wants us to do, we can be certain there will
be consequences.

Learn from Saul. To obey God is more important
than any sacrifice we can make. ■

Broken Ranks

The Spirit clearly says that in later times some will abandon the faith and follow deceiving spirits and things taught by demons.
(1 Timothy 4:1)

Unfortunately, military history contains instances where some have "broken ranks" and joined the enemy. Whatever the reasons, the outcomes for those who disobeyed have met with disaster most of the time.

One such incident occurred on April 28, 1779, when crewmembers of the HMS Bounty mutinied against Lt. William Bligh, the ship's captain. Of the 45 members of the British Navy aboard the vessel, 26 of them joined Fletcher Christian, leader of the mutiny. But for the mutineers who broke ranks, most died prematurely through violent death, some by hanging.

Sadly, history also records that some soldiers in God's army have also "broken ranks" with God. Some will even do so in the future.

Be smart. Don't be deceived by the enemy of your soul. Stay in God's camp. If you have "broken ranks," confess your sin to your Heavenly Commander, receive His forgiveness, and spend eternity in His presence. ■

Walking with God

This is the account of Noah. Noah was a righteous man, blameless among the people of his time, and he walked with God.
(Genesis 6:9)

Can this be said about you? If not, why not?

Before you answer, please understand that walking with God doesn't mean perfection. Later in the same chapter of Genesis, we learn that Noah drank wine from fruit planted in his vineyard and became drunk.

The meaning of this verse is that Noah was a man who did his best to follow God. He is most famous for obeying God's command to build an ark, but Noah tried to submit to God's ways on a daily basis. Because of his commitment, the Lord commends him in Scripture.

Many times, walking with God simply means doing what you know is the right thing. Do this in marriage, in handling money, and in the way you do your job.

As Commander in Chief of our universe, God is looking for people who are willing to be soldiers in His army and walk with Him in obedience.

Walking with God is not a matter of capability or feeling. It's a decision. ∎

Submitting to Your Commander

Once made perfect, he became the source of eternal salvation for all who obey him.
(Hebrews 5:9)

The presence of great leadership does not guarantee that an army will be victorious. The followers must listen and carry out the orders of those in authority.

In fact, obedience is so important that a soldier wanting to reenlist must swear or affirm that he will obey the orders of the president of the United States as well as the orders of the officers appointed over him.

On the spiritual battlefield the rules work the same way. If we are going to triumph over our enemy, the Devil, we must first submit to our Commander. The Lord knows all about the rules for victory. He wrote them.

Ironically, most military men and women obey their leaders, contributing significantly to a mission accomplishment. Yet somehow, they approach submission to God in a half-hearted manner. Does this make sense?

Dying on a cross was serious commitment. It required Jesus' total submission. But through His obedience, Jesus Christ became the sacrifice for our sins and the source of our eternal salvation.

Are you fully submitting to Him? ■

Walking in His Light

In him was life, and that was the light of men.
(John 1.4)

Night-fighting capabilities are no longer optional. Technological advances demand that commanders train units in the effective use of night vision devices on today's lethal battlefield. We are doing this very effectively in Iraq and Afghanistan.

Most of the time insurgents don't possess good night-fighting equipment. Foolishly, they have tested U. S. forces during the hours of darkness and discovered a deadly truth. On the physical battlefield, those walking in darkness cannot compete with those who walk in the light.

Ironically, some soldiers still resist. They would rather trust their natural vision. This could be tragic — human abilities alone are no match for an enemy that employs night vision technology skillfully.

Spiritual warfare is much like fighting at night. Those with the ability to see the spiritual battlefield clearly can locate and defeat the enemy of our souls. Those without good spiritual vision walk around in the dark and present themselves as easy targets for the enemy.

Jesus Christ is the Light we need to wage and win in spiritual warfare. Are you walking in His light? ∎

Following Orders

Jesus answered, "If I want him to remain alive until I return, what is that to you? You must follow me."
(John 21:22)

Good soldiers follow orders. They follow orders because it is part of military order and discipline, and because they trust their leaders.

But even the best soldiers struggle when they don't understand the rationale behind the orders or they believe the orders are unjust.

Now here is the challenging part. Sometimes leaders are able to share the bigger picture and explain the "why" behind the orders. But other times, they are not. In these cases, the followers must simply trust the judgment of their leaders.

This verse contains Jesus' response to Peter when Peter felt that God was showing preferential treatment toward another disciple — John. Did Jesus apologize? No! In direct language Jesus told Peter not to worry about John, but simply to obey His order: "Follow me!"

Peter obeyed. It was a smart move on his part.

Are you arguing with God, or have you decided to obey His order? Jesus said, "Follow me." ∎

Not in My Strength

"For God so loved the world that he gave his one and only Son, that whoever believes in him shall not perish but have eternal life."
(John 3:16)

To simply call Christianity a religion is to completely misunderstand it. True Christianity is about a relationship — relationship with God through His Son Jesus Christ. Following Jesus begins with believing that He came to save the world. Through His death on the cross, He paid the penalty for our sins — past, present and future.

Although God created the world and everything in it and He loves us unconditionally. He doesn't force us to believe in Him or serve Him. He gives every person a free will. Though Christ's death at Calvary and His resurrection almost 2,000 years ago were for all people, God leaves the choice to us as to whether we will accept Christ as Savior. The choice is ours. But we are not free from the consequences of our choice.

John 3:16, the verse quoted above, states a wonderful truth. Believing in Jesus gives us access into eternal life with God. Two verses down in the same passage, Jesus speaks these sobering words:

"Whoever believes in him is not condemned, but whoever does not believe stands condemned already because he has not believed in the name of God's one and only Son."
(John 3:18)

Ironically, many people do not realize how straightforwardly Scripture states the need for salvation through Jesus. The Bible also speaks clearly about the distinction between believers and nonbelievers concerning where they will spend eternity. I'm even talking about people who go to church regularly.

I will use myself as a good example. I wasn't much a churchgoer for the first 24 years of my life. Even when I did go to church, I don't remember hearing the need for salvation expressed in any of the preaching.

A Christian minister asked me a straightforward question during a premarital counseling session: "Scott, do you know Jesus Christ as your personal Savior?"

My response? I was absolutely clueless and asked the minister to explain. He did, and two days later I committed my life to Christ. I have never looked back.

Am I the only one who just didn't get it? Unfortunately, there are many in our world who don't yet understand Jesus' offer of salvation. It's imperative for someone to tell them. I'm so grateful that the minister took an interest in me and in where I will spend eternity. Since that time, I've tried to spread the message to others.

In the fall of 1989, I was stationed in Seoul, Korea, for a two-year tour. Fortunately, my family was there with me. I was serving as the pastor for Hannam Village, the largest U.S. government housing area in Korea with a population approaching 4,500 military personnel and their families. One day I was working out at the gym on main post and met a senior noncommissioned officer named Frank Miller who was also working out. We struck up a conversation, and I learned he had spent a lot of time in Vietnam as a member of Special Forces.

Over the next few months we would see each other frequently at the gym. As we got to know one another better, I felt comfortable in asking him about his faith. He mentioned that he had been raised in the Far East and had a faith that was a blend of several major religions. He made it clear from the beginning that he was very comfortable with his religion and that if he ever wanted help he'd let me know. Bottom line: He really didn't want to talk about it. I understood, but still made an effort to continue our friendship.

Several months went by. One Friday night while I was conducting a wedding rehearsal at Hannam Village Chapel, my chaplain assistant interrupted the rehearsal to tell me a man was on the phone who really needed some help. The assistant persuaded me to take the call. It was Frank Miller, and he was crying and very distraught. I made arrangements to meet him in about two hours at a 24-hour snack bar on main post.

I met Frank at the snack bar, and he explained the situation. His wife was leaving him and would not be dissuaded. She lived in Hawaii at the time. He told me he had never encountered such a challenge. He had served four years in Vietnam with Special Forces and had been wounded several times, but somehow had survived. Now he faced a situation that left him feeling powerless.

"I don't have anything in my arsenal to cope with my marriage falling apart," he said to me. "Can you help me?"

I told Frank that I knew Someone who could help. I spoke to Frank about Jesus. Although Frank previously was not open to hearing about spiritual matters, now he was desperate and listened to every word. I explained what Jesus had done for him and how Jesus loved him unconditionally. I told Frank that Jesus wanted a relationship with him and what Frank could do to enter into a relationship.

Despite dozens of other people seated at surrounding tables, Frank expressed a strong desire to pray and ask Jesus into his life. I led Frank in prayer. At the conclusion Frank became a Christian, and he knew it. His countenance changed dramatically, and it was easy to tell that God had lifted a huge burden from Frank.

Some military people think they don't need God and that they are strong enough to stand on their own. Frank Miller thought that for a long time. Humanly speaking, Frank could justify his self-dependence more than most. He was the winner of the Congressional Medal of Honor for his bravery in Vietnam.

But even this war hero finally saw that he was not strong enough to stand without the Lord. How about you? ■

Bad News, Good News

Here is a trustworthy saying that deserves full acceptance: Christ Jesus came into the world to save sinners — of whom I am the worst.
(1 Timothy 1:15)

Most soldiers know the truth when they hear it. In this verse the apostle Paul tells Timothy the most profound truth any person could ever hear. He tells it in two parts — bad news and good news.

The bad news: Paul says there are sinners in the world, and he is the worst. In fact, the Bible tells us that all of us are sinners and fall short of God's glory. Within the entire human race, there is not one exception — not one.

The good news: The bad news is not hopeless. Jesus Christ came to save sinners, even Paul. The blood of Jesus covers every sin, yours included!

Two major misunderstandings generally surface about this bad news and good news. First, some think they are not sinners. Bad mistake! Second, others think they have done too many bad things and can't be forgiven. This is also not true.

But what have you done with this truth — both the bad and the good? Have you trusted Christ as your personal Savior? ∎

Saved Through Acceptance

This is good, and pleases God our Savior, who wants all men to be saved and to come to a knowledge of the truth.
(1 Timothy 2:3,4)

Good leaders are motivated by a sincere concern for the welfare of all soldiers under their command. No leaders worth their salt can think differently.

With nearly seven billion souls on this planet, it seems utterly impossible for us as humans to care deeply about every single person. Truthfully, it can seem hard to care about a nearby neighbor whom you don't know. Even more difficult is caring about people who don't like you or who have mistreated you.

Thankfully, the Lord doesn't struggle with our human limitations. God, as Commander-in-Chief over all creation, loves every single person around this world. This includes you.

The Lord cares enough to tell you the truth. Though your sins have separated you from God, the truth is that you can be saved through your acceptance of His Son, Jesus Christ.

The ball is in your court. Have you accepted Him as your Savior? ∎

Taking the Right Step

*"Yet as surely as the L*ORD* lives and as you live, there is only a step between me and death."*
(1 Samuel 20:3)

David's words spoken to Jonathan 3,000 years ago still hold true. The distance between life and death can be as short as a single step.

Soldiers know this — especially airborne soldiers. One step is the difference between the safety of the aircraft and the danger of falling out hundreds of feet above the ground. The key is being ready.

Not long ago, a friend of mine bought his first motorcycle and was riding it in his neighborhood. He suddenly lost control and crashed into an oncoming car. He died instantly. In his zeal to ride his new motorcycle, he had failed to prepare properly and lost his life.

Physical death is certain, but where we spend eternity is not. Jesus Christ has conquered death and provided the way to eternal life. But where you spend eternity depends on taking the right step.

Jesus has promised to receive all who believe in Him into heaven to spend eternity with Him.

Are you ready? Have you taken the step to receive Him? ■

Living Water

Jesus answered, "Everyone who drinks this water will be thirsty again, but whoever drinks the water I give him will never thirst. Indeed, the water I give him will become in him a spring of water welling up to eternal life."
(John 4:13,14)

Logistical preparations for military operations must always include a plan for water. Water sustains human life. Leaders know that water is not an option — it's a necessity.

As in infantry platoon leader in Vietnam, I always relied on my non-commissioned officers to make certain our troops had sufficient water. The mission just couldn't happen without it. From experience, they knew the critical importance of water and never failed to provide it. Never.

Just as there is no physical life without water, Jesus tells the Samaritan woman that there is no spiritual life without the Living Water He alone provides. That Living Water is the Holy Spirit whom Jesus gives to all believe in Him.

Some say they're just fine without this Living Water. Jesus says otherwise. We should trust his experience.

What do you say? Do you have this Living Water? Remember, we need to plan for eternity. Eternity is a long time. ■

ENDEX

*"No one knows about that day or hour, not even the
angels in heaven, nor the Son, but only the Father.
Be on guard! Be alert! You do not know
when that time will come."*
(Mark 13:32,33)

In military training vernacular, ENDEX is an
acronym that means "end of exercise." Usually, the
time for ENDEX is announced before the exercise
even begins because the military must stick to a tight
schedule. Normally soldiers like to hear that word
because intense training halts and people can relax.

In God's Word, there is promise of an "ENDEX" of
far greater magnitude — the Second Coming of Jesus
Christ. Life as we have known it on earth will cease.

For those who are ready, it will be a joyous reunion
with our Lord, a reunion that will last for eternity.
For those who are unprepared, it will be a time of
unspeakable disaster.

When will "ENDEX" occur? Jesus himself says that
only the Father knows when "ENDEX" will come. But
He also tells us we must be ready.

Are you prepared to meet the Lord? If not, don't
delay. Don't gamble with your soul. ■

The Lord's Army

*I saw heaven standing open and there before me
was a white horse, whose rider is called Faithful and
True. With justice he judges and makes war. . . .
The armies of heaven were following him, riding on
white horses and dressed in fine linen,
white and clean.*
(Revelation 19:11,14)

For troops fighting in intensive combat, few things
are sweeter than knowing that the commander is about
to commit reinforcements that will ensure victory over
a fierce enemy.

This verse begins a passage that describes just that.
At some future time, our Commander in Chief of this
universe, Jesus Christ, will ride to earth on a white
horse leading the armies of heaven into one final
engagement.

The outcome of the fight? Verse 15 leaves no doubt:
"Out of his mouth comes a sharp sword with which
to strike down the nations." This heavenly army will
crush the enemy.

Should you be afraid? It depends on whose army
you're in. If you haven't enlisted yet, why don't you
join the Lord's army today? There is a place for
you! ■

Safety in God

If you make the Most High your dwelling — even the LORD, who is my refuge — then no harm will befall you, no disaster will come near your tent. (Psalm 91:9,10)

According to Army doctrine, the conduct of defensive operations requires taking the initiative. Defending is not passive.

Commanders of units who successfully defend against enemy attack take the initiative in carrying out the fundamentals of defense: preparation, disruption, concentration and flexibility. Merely sitting back and waiting for the enemy to attack invites disaster.

During the Vietnam conflict, the enemy would occasionally overrun U. S. firebases. They did this with inferior weapons and equipment. How? Poor defensive positions, improperly strung wire, and shortages of early warning devices all contributed to weaknesses that the enemy exploited.

On the spiritual battlefield, the devil wages continuous offensive operations against your soul. He aim is to kill, steal and destroy. Can you successfully defend?

Yes! But don't sit back and wait for the enemy to attack. Seize the initiative! Make the Most High your dwelling. No disaster will come near your tent! ■

Onward, Christian Soldier!

Be on your guard; stand firm in the faith;
be men of courage; be strong.
(1 Corinthians 16:13)

In a world containing nearly seven billion people, we may be tempted to underestimate the influence of a single life. Last year provided me a vivid reminder of just how great a difference one person can make.

On Thursday, April 24, 2008, I received news that 1LT Tim Cunningham died in Iraq the day prior. He was serving with the 101st Airborne Division out of Fort Campbell, Ky. The death of this 26-year-old infantry officer from Texas left my family and me stunned. In the three years that we knew him at West Point, Tim had a profound impact on the McChrystal family, on the staff and faculty, and on hundreds of his fellow cadets.

Tim entered West Point in the summer of 2002, just one month after his older brother, John David, had graduated from the same institution. I met Tim during cadet basic training and quickly saw him as a most impressive and caring young man. I also noted that he signed up to teach children's Sunday School, an activity he did all four years at West Point. During two of those years, one of his Sunday School students was our youngest son, Josh. Josh is now a cadet at West Point and fondly remembers the genuine interest that Tim had shown in him. Tim not only taught Josh about Jesus, he also modeled the Christian life in a quiet and credible fashion. Tim truly loved Josh, and Josh knew it. Josh had e-mailed back and forth with Tim only days before Tim's death.

It's appropriate for people to say nice things about a person who has died, particularly a young patriot who gave his life for the defense of his country. It's even better when the things said are true. In Tim's case, they are. Rev. Alfred Perry of First Baptist Church in Rosharon, Texas, where Tim's father is music minister, said this: "He was the type of young man that makes you proud to be an American." I couldn't agree more.

What made Tim Cunningham such an impressive and influential young man? The answer is simply that Tim stood strong for the Lord in all places at all times. His influence extended far beyond his family and fellow cadets at the United States Military Academy. His stand for the Lord profoundly touched the people of Iraq.

A few weeks after Tim's death, his brother, John, returned to Iraq to complete his tour as an engineer company commander with the 101st Airborne Division.

Standing Strong

He ran into Tim's brigade commander one day who passed along some amazing information about Tim concerning Golden Hills, an area just north of Baghdad.

The commander told John that he had been talking to some Iraqi tribal leaders in the Golden Hills area, Tim's area of operations, soon after Tim's passing. He said the Iraqis talked about "Mulazem Tim," and the great job he was doing there — they didn't yet know what had happened. When the commander broke the news about Tim's death, he said that they broke down crying.

The commander shared that he frequently had talked to Iraqi families who had lost sons as the result of firefights, and their reactions often seemed indifferent and unaffected. With Tim, an American, it was different. They broke down and wept aloud.

But that wasn't all. He asked John, "Do you know what is going down in Golden Hills now?"

John answered, "No, sir, I don't."

The commander reported that 200 Iraqi men there had turned themselves in for reconciliation. Formerly these guys were fighting against the United States. But because of the work Tim had done with them, they now wanted to lay down their arms and join our side.

How could a young man make such a strong stand for the Lord? The answer lies embedded in a note Tim left on his computer before he deployed to Iraq. He had erased everything else from his hard drive except for a set of instructions to be read in case he was wounded, captured or killed.

If I die in a combat zone . . .

Please follow all instructions in my green book. I am okay. I have been redeemed by the Lord of hosts, the Commander of the Lord's Army, the one who will chain the serpent and all his servants, my Savior Jesus Christ.

Have a memorial celebration where the message of the Gospel is clear and please Read 1Cor 15:57[,58] at some point in the service.

To my platoon . . .

See for yourselves that men don't need to be gruff, tough and brave to be considered a man. The real men are those that seek to lose their own inhibitions, failures and sin, and choose to follow a higher order. I choose to follow Christ. I will always lose myself and follow Him. If I am spent, it is because I have completed all that He wanted me to accomplish, and have been called home. You are all fine men, and I am proud to have been near you in combat, and I consider each one of you friends.

Farewells and things left unsaid . . .

I love my family more than anything on earth. To think that I will never see you again pains my heart. But I take courage in knowing that the Lord has gone before us to plan a way for us. He has crossed over from death to life to lead us to our new Home. I pray I will see all of you there.

Lieutenant Tim Cunningham stood strong for the Lord until the day he died. By placing your faith in Jesus Christ, you can demonstrate that same strength. It's your choice. Choose Christ. ∎

Spiritual Fitness

For physical training is of some value, but godliness has value for all things, holding promise for both the present life and the life to come.
(1 Timothy 4:8)

Few know the value of PT (physical training) more than the soldier. Being "fit to fight" can make the difference between winning and losing — between living and dying.

But physical fitness is not enough by itself. Paul, a seasoned veteran in the Lord's army, warned a younger soldier named Timothy that godliness is even more important than PT.

Why? PT applies to this life only. Godliness holds promise, now and for the future — even through eternity.

Spiritual fitness also has huge impact on this life. Want proof? Consider the number of very physically fit soldiers who have returned from Iraq and Afghanistan, but who are still experiencing mega problems back in the States. Tragically, some have even turned to suicide as the answer.

Spiritual fitness can be very effective toward maintaining good mental and emotional health. Many soldiers have relied on faith in God to handle difficult problems.

Bottom line: Stay physically fit, but don't be shortsighted. Make spiritual training a part of your routine. It will pay eternal rewards! ■

Fit to Fight

Finally, be strong in the Lord and in his mighty power.
(Ephesians 6.10)

Battles, and even wars, can be won or lost based on which side is most "fit to fight." Fitness encompasses not only physical and mental strength, but spiritual strength as well.

Some 3,000 years ago a Philistine giant named Goliath engaged a young shepherd named David in a fight to the death. Standing more than 9 feet tall and many times David's match in physical strength, Goliath seemed to be the sure victor. But David didn't think of the battle as his own.

David voiced his assurance this way: "You come against me with sword and spear and javelin, but I come against you in the name of the LORD Almighty, the God of the armies of Israel, whom you have defied" (1 Samuel 17:45).

Far too many wonderful military men and women are losing battles in their personal lives- divorces, financial problems, life-controlling habits- simply because they are battling in their own strength.

How are you fighting the "Goliaths" in your life? Are you battling in your own strength, or are you strong in the Lord? ■

Spiritual Battlefield

*Put on the full armor of God so that you can take
your stand against the devil's schemes.
(Ephesians 6:11)*

In combat, no smart soldier fails to utilize all available
protection. The modern battlefield is too lethal to do
otherwise.

One of the pluses coming out of the global war
on terrorism is the large number of U. S. forces who
are surviving potentially lethal blows by enemy fire,
mortars and IEDs (Improvised Explosive Devices)
because of the protective equipment they utilize.
Amazingly, many soldiers have even survived sniper
rounds to the head because of the outstanding
protective capabilities of their helmets.

The spiritual battlefield is no different. We face a
deadly enemy whose aim is to steal, kill and destroy.
His name is Satan. But the Lord assures us that we can
stand against the devil's schemes — if we put on the
whole armor of God.

But note one important fact on both battlefields,
physical and spiritual: Soldiers must wear the armor. It
is useless if not worn.

Are you wearing the full armor of God? If not,
put it on! ■

Armor of God

Therefore put on the full armor of God, so that when the day of evil comes, you may be able to stand your ground, and after you have done everything, to stand.
(Ephesians 6:13)

The Lord admonishes us to use all of the spiritual armor He makes available.

Why? As with any formidable enemy, the devil is a skillful tactician and strategist who wants to attack at our weakest point. Failure to wear the full armor leaves us vulnerable, and almost guarantees we will become casualties on the deadly battlefield of spiritual combat.

Consider this example: In Iraq and Afghanistan, soldiers are routinely having prayer before launching convoys on the dangerous roads and highways. The good news is that this spiritual weapon is working and the Lord is protecting our forces.

Unfortunately, many soldiers make good use of the military weapons on the battlefield, but neglect to use the spiritual weapons that the Lord has provided for battles in their personal lives. It doesn't have to be this way. The Lord can help.

What about you? Do you know how to put on the armor of God? Are you putting it on daily? ∎

Standing through Truth

Stand firm then, with the belt of truth buckled around your waist, with the breastplate of righteousness in place.
(Ephesians 6:14)

On the modern battlefield, commanders employ many intelligence-gathering systems to gain "ground truth." They need accurate information with which to make sound tactical decisions. Good decisions save lives.

Spiritually speaking, knowing the truth is even more crucial. Why? The only part of life that crosses the threshold between this world and the next is the human soul. Eternity is a long time. Where you spend it hinges on knowing the truth.

In the information age in which we live, some would argue that there is no such thing as absolute truth. One reason they make this claim is they don't want to be accountable. If there is no such thing as absolute truth, then they are free to choose their own version of truth.

But God didn't design life this way. God is truth and his Word is truth. Truth about God and life can be known. Read his Word!

Spiritually speaking, are you standing firm with the belt of truth buckled around your waist?

The stakes are too high to do otherwise. ∎

Standing Strong

Training in Prayer

And pray in the Spirit on all occasions with all kinds of prayers and requests. With this in mind, be alert and always keep on praying for all the saints. (Ephesians 6:18)

According to Army doctrine, "battle focus" is a concept used to derive peacetime training requirements from wartime missions.

Given the growing resource constraints being imposed on the military community, leaders must focus on training those tasks that are critical for the unit's mission in wartime. There just isn't the time and money for everything.

Battle focus is essential in the Christian life as well. With the fast pace that most of us keep, it is critical that we train on those tasks essential for our spiritual wartime mission.

Our Heavenly Commander has identified prayer as a cornerstone of spiritual warfare doctrine. Every soldier in the Lord's army must train in prayer. It is a spiritual weapon so powerful that the enemy goes all out to stop it. Prayer demolishes enemy strongholds.

Life is hard. Stay battle-focused. Pray hard and pray often. ■

Resist the Devil

Submit yourselves, then, to God. Resist the devil,
and he will flee from you.
(James 4:7)

Imagine a battalion-sized task force of 600 soldiers preparing to defend against an anticipated attack by a fierce and well-prepared enemy with forces outnumbering theirs.

What would happen if each soldier independently prepared and executed his own battle plan without regard for the task force commander's battle plan? Not much doubt about the outcome — disaster with a big "D."

As absurd as this example seems, many people try to wage spiritual warfare against the devil without any regard for our Heavenly Commander's commands or guidance. Result? They get repeatedly steamrolled.

It is important to mention that in today's culture, a lot of people don't believe that the devil even exists. This would explain their lack of motivation for submitting to God. If there is no enemy, what's the problem?

But consider the evidence. Beside the fact Jesus taught that the devil exists, take a look at our world. The devil definitely exists, and he's working overtime!

So what can you do? Submit to God first. Then resist the devil and watch him flee. ■

Faithful to the End

For I know that through your prayers and the help given by the Spirit of Jesus Christ, what has happened to me will turn out for my deliverance. I eagerly expect and hope that I will in no way be ashamed, but will have sufficient courage so that now as always Christ will be exalted in my body, whether by life or by death. For to me, to live is Christ and to die is gain.
(Philippians 1:19-21)

On a muggy summer morning at West Point, New York, the starting gun sounded for a 10K race. The course stretched over some hilly terrain. Even the best conditioned athletes would be tested to their limits.

Slightly over 30 minutes later, the first runners appeared and soon crossed the finish line. None of the competitors looked exuberant. The combination of heat and humidity was taking its toll. Numerous runners had to drop out. Others straggled across the finish line. The medical aid tent rapidly filled up with participants who had overdone it. Many were dehydrated and were given IVs.

As more and more runners came to the medical tent, I dropped the idea of watching the remainder of the race. As the Academy chaplain, I knew these exhausted runners needed my full attention.

As I continued to visit and pray with people, I came across a young Army major by the name of John Roseborough. Admittedly, I was very surprised to see him needing medical attention because he was so superbly fit. As they tended to John, somehow the IV fluid didn't seem to make much difference. The attending doctor sent John by ambulance to the Keller Army Hospital ER. They wound up keeping him for four days in an effort to determine the reason John was experiencing excruciating pain in his abdomen. They performed a colonoscopy and found a large mass in his colon. It was cancer of the most aggressive kind.

The day of the race was August 28, 1999. Over the coming months, I had the privilege of being pastor to John, his wife, Sontil, and their little son, Brandon. John bravely underwent chemotherapy and radiation, and for a while, it seemed as though the cancer was diminishing. During these months John continued to work most of the time and even did physical training.

After almost 18 months, the cancer returned with a vengeance. It was evident that only a miracle would save John's life. But throughout his ordeal, I never heard John utter one complaint. I never heard him say anything but how much he loved God and was trusting Him for his healing. Defeat was not in John's vocabulary

By March 2001, the end was near. The cancer had spread throughout John's body, causing enormous pain. John was sent home to die in his apartment on the grounds of West Point. To make it through the incessant pain, the doctors had him medicated with high dosages of morphine. Much of the time, John just slept. When awake, he lapsed in and out of consciousness.

On Thursday, March 8, I informed Lieutenant General Dan Christman, Superintendant of the Military Academy, about John's condition and advised him that if he wanted to see John alive, it needed to be soon. We made an appointment for later that same day.

As we walked across the street and headed up the stairs to John's apartment, I warned General Christman that I did not know what to expect. There was a chance John would not be conscious. And even if he was, that he might not be able to speak. General Christman and I were both in for a surprise.

We knocked on the door, expecting Sontil to answer. Instead, it was Major John Roseborough standing at the position of attention. He greeted us warmly and rendered a crisp salute to the superintendent. We had a great visit, amazed by the strength, courage and faith of the young major.

Two days later, I went to visit John. Sontil told me he was lying in his bed. I could see tears forming in her eyes, so I knew things were not looking good. As she led me into his bedroom, I was surprised at how bad John looked. Cancer is a cruel disease. I had spent time with dying cancer patients previously, and John's appearance matched my previous experiences. Death was clearly knocking at his door.

The only other person in the room was John's brother who had only traveled to West Point in the last few hours and had just arrived to their apartment a few minutes before I got there. Apparently, the brothers hadn't seen much of each other over the past several years, and it was not looking hopeful that they would be able to have any meaningful communication before John passed.

John's brother was not a person of faith and needed some assurance about what was happening to his own flesh and blood. I desperately wanted to provide John's brother with encouragement, but couldn't find the words. I simply prayed.

Setting the Example

Finally, as I began to speak to his brother, John suddenly sat up in his bed. He looked his brother in the eye and gave a thumbs up. Without words, he was telling his brother that everything was OK. God would take good care of him. A huge sigh of relief came over the face of John's brother. God's presence at that moment was undeniable. I will never forget that moment.

After a few more minutes, I knew it was time for me to leave so that John's brother, Sontil, and their son could be there alone with John. I planned to return a few hours later. Less than two hours after I left, John went to be with the Lord.

Setting the example is important. Major John Roseborough set the example in how he lived for Christ. He also set the example in his death. He showed his faith until the end. I am looking forward to seeing John in heaven. ■

Up for the Challenge

*Don't let anyone look down on you because you
are young, but set an example for the believers in
speech, in life, in love, in faith and in purity.*
(1 Timothy 4:12)

Leadership by example is critically important within
the military. Think back on those leaders who have set
the kind of example you were proud to follow.

Setting the right example extends beyond the "high
viz" kinds of leadership techniques that may win
immediate applause from troops. It means more than
doing the right thing when things are going well.
Setting a good example necessitates doing the right
thing even when the going gets tough or the decision is
unpopular.

God not only challenges leaders to set the example
in the visible areas of life, but also in important areas
such as speech, lifestyle, love, faith and purity.

As you set the example, be sure there are others
watching and learning. They may be troops under your
control, or they may be family members like a spouse
or children.

The fact is you are always setting the example. The
question is this: what kind of example are you setting? ■

God's Command

Dear friend, do not imitate what is evil but what is good. Anyone who does what is good is from God. Anyone who does what is evil has not seen God.
(3 John 1:11)

Many of us would agree that a lot of what we see in America today is not good. Almost everywhere we turn we see examples of how things should not be.

As military men and women, can we use the excuse that "everyone else is doing it"? God says we are not to imitate the evil we see, but rather to imitate that which is good.

Are you taking God's command seriously? In your everyday life in the military, are you setting the right example? Your actions don't affect just you. Others may imitate what you do.

Consider this small example. At public restaurants, some Christians pray just like they do at home. Others don't. Why? Because they are more concerned about what others may think than they are about following God. Imitating God sometimes takes courage.

And remember, it is not only your reputation at stake. God's name is honored or shamed by what you say and do. ∎

A Few Good Men

*He was a good man, full of the Holy Spirit and faith,
and a great number of people were
brought to the Lord.
(Acts 11:24)*

This verse describes a man named Barnabas who lived during the early days of the Christian Church. Although he was a man with leadership skills and multiple talents, he seems to be best remembered for being a good man who consistently put the needs of others ahead of his own. Barnabas was truly a good person, not only because he brought many people to faith in Christ, but also because he was always enabling others to reach their full potential.

In the rat race of military life, isn't it refreshing to see good leaders who, like Barnabas, enable others to succeed?

The U. S. Marine Corps isn't alone in its search for a few good men. God is searching for men and women who will serve Him faithfully and draw others to faith in Him.

God continues to search. If you have yet to commit yourself to Him, He is certainly trying to recruit you for His team. ■

Honor His Name

You shall not misuse the name of the LORD your God, for the LORD will not hold anyone guiltless who misuses his name.
(Deuteronomy 5:11)

Taking the Lord's name in vain is commonplace among the military. But just because others do it, does that mean you have to?

God's Word is clear: We are to honor His name.

Over 30 years ago, an infantry company commander stood in front of his men. Some soldier had stolen a privately owned weapon from another soldier, but no one would step forward and provide any info. In a burst of anger, the officer cursed God's name in front of the entire formation. The captain was a professing Christian.

Decades later I recall that moment like it was yesterday. Why? I was that young officer. While the Lord has forgiven me, it has made a lasting impression. I love the Lord and want others to love Him as well because of the way I honor Him.

Perhaps you can identify. Starting now, why don't you ask the Lord for help in doing just that.

Honor His name! ∎

Trash Talk

Do not let any unwholesome talk come out of your mouths, but only what is helpful for building others up according to their needs, that it may benefit those who listen.
(Ephesians 4:29)

Military leaders at all levels spend huge amounts of time communicating with other people. If this is true and you are a leader, doesn't it make sense to develop your communications skills to a high degree?

This Scripture sets forth a powerful mandate toward better communication, but certainly one easier said than done. Take a close look at the verse again and think about what it's saying.

No unwholesome talk. Use words to build others up. Benefit others by what we say.

Doesn't the bottom line tell us to omit trashy, destructive kinds of speech and start using language that will meet the needs of others by building them up?

You ask, "Can this really work in the military?" Of course it can. You can communicate any message required and be as hard as woodpecker lips without using profanity or tearing a fellow soldier down.

But you'll never know for yourself until you try it. ■

Credible Leadership

In the same way, faith by itself, if it is not accompanied by action, is dead.
(James 2:17)

For leadership to be effective, it must be credible. Leaders must say what they mean and mean what they say.

Leadership doesn't end with the spoken word, however. Soldiers look for their leaders' actions to back up their words. If leaders fail in this essential task, their credibility goes down the tube.

One of the acid tests of credible leadership is leaders' willingness to share the hardships that their soldiers face. Troops want to follow leaders who are willing to be with them during hard or dangerous times.

In the same way, our walk with God must have faith with works. If we claim to have great faith in God, how do those around us know if this is true?

One way is how we use our time. Do we take time to serve others? Another is our handling of money. Do we hoard it just for ourselves, or do we look for ways to help those in need?

If you want your faith to be credible, back it up with action! ∎

It's All about Team

Who will listen to what you say? The share of the man who stayed with the supplies is to be the same as that of him who went down to the battle. All will share alike.
(1 Samuel 30:24)

King David was a great military leader who knew the importance of teamwork in winning battles. He recognized that the elements of combat, combat support, and combat service support must work together if Israel was to be victorious.

When members of his army recommended that rear-echelon soldiers not be given a share of the booty captured as the Israelites defeated the Amalekites, David vetoed the recommendation. He gave a share to every soldier.

In society today, there is a strong tendency to promote self. But promoting self is a bad tactic. Life is about teamwork. There is an old saying that applies here: "When you see a frog on the top of a flagpole, rest assured he did not get there by himself!"

Lesson learned: Your contribution is important. But so is the contribution of other soldiers with different responsibilities. Give your fellow soldiers the credit and respect they deserve. ∎

The Buck Stops Here

*Do nothing out of selfish ambition or vain conceit,
but in humility consider others better than
yourselves.*
(Philippians 2:3)

Realistic training for combat can have many moving
parts and tends to get complicated fast. This is especially
true when using live ammunition. Leaders know they
must fashion good plans, issue clear orders, and delegate
authority in order for missions to succeed. Ultimately,
however, responsibility falls on the shoulders of the
senior leader.

Mixed in with this is the issue of safety. Training
needs to tax the troops to the limit, but there is a line
that shouldn't be crossed in order to avoid unnecessary
casualties. Risk assessment is not easy.

In spite of all precautions, stuff happens. Things go
wrong and people get hurt or killed. Times like this
reveal a lot about the leaders. Competent and caring
leaders step in and take charge. They want to take all
the necessary steps to rectify the situation and take
care of troops. Self-serving leaders tend to go into a
defensive mode in order to protect themselves. Blaming
others is a frequent tactic. They want to protect their
careers at all costs.

In the early 1970s I belonged
to a unit that deployed to a
Caribbean island for an important
training exercise. I was placed
in charge of the rear deployment
while the unit deployed for approximately two
weeks.

Things seemed to be running smoothly.
Daily I would receive reports about the
training. Late one evening, however, I received
a disturbing report that a serious training
accident had occurred in which several soldiers
had been killed or wounded.

During a live-fire exercise in which mortar
rounds were being fired, a number of rounds
hit in the vicinity of soldiers as they moved on foot to
the objective. Evidently, a mistake resulted in rounds
being shot onto the wrong location. It was a tragic
incident in which "friendly fire" proved fatal.

The unit took all the necessary steps to evacuate the
wounded quickly and get them to proper medical care.
Unfortunately, several soldiers didn't make it.

Back at Fort Bragg we initiated action to notify
family members of soldiers killed or wounded. We took
extra precautions to disseminate information quickly,

but accurately. Bad information in cases like this only compounds the problems.

The division headquarters sent safety experts to join the unit to conduct a thorough investigation of the circumstances surrounding the training accident. They interviewed dozens of people, gathered hundreds of pages of depositions, and took all measures necessary toward determining the causes of the deadly incident. The unit returned, but the investigation continued for weeks after the troops had arrived back at home station.

From the first day that the unit returned, I heard a lot of talk about the accident from leaders and soldiers at all levels. Understandably, there was much speculation as to where the mistakes had actually occurred. No one person had all of the information, and everyone anxiously awaited the report from the investigation. The report would likely find the causes for the accident and affix responsibility for the mishap. Most likely, those assigned the blame would face serious consequences.

Human nature kicked in quickly as the speculation continued. I heard some leaders talking in ways to protect themselves and their careers. They rehearsed repeatedly the measures they had taken to insure that the exercise had gone safely. I didn't hear anyone even hint that they might have contributed to the accident.

After several more weeks, word traveled throughout the unit that the report was final and rested in the hands of the division Commander for final review. But then an interesting thing happened. Before top leaders released any specifics from the investigation, our battalion commander stepped forward publicly and accepted responsibility for the incident. He stated that since he was the senior leader on the ground, he rightfully was responsible for everything that happened or failed to happen. In effect, he said, "The buck stops here."

The hammer didn't take long to fall. Our battalion commander was relieved for the incident and moved to another duty assignment. To my knowledge, no other officer or noncommissioned officer received punishment for the accident. The senior leader took the entire brunt of the punishment on his shoulders. It seemed unfair. Yes, he deserved a measure of punishment, but not all of it!

Caring for Others

I remember my amazement that this man would step up and take the entire blame without trying to fault others. Unlike some less senior leaders in the unit, he demonstrated courage and accountability for his actions. Perhaps most inspiring of all, he showed more concern for others than for himself. In spite of the negative impact on his own life and career, He chose to sacrifice himself that others would not have to pay.

Decades have passed and I still think about this leader often. He has my utmost respect and admiration. I can also tell you this about him. I would serve under him again — any time, any place. He's a leader I can follow.

Does this sound like any other leader you know? Almost 2,000 years ago, Jesus Christ descended from heaven in the form of a man. He surrendered his divinity to become like us. He came and showed us how to live. More amazingly, he came to die for our sins so that the Father's judgment for our sins would not fall on us.

To put it more directly, Jesus died for your sins and for mine. And He has asked us to follow Him.

Will you? ∎

More Than Just Noise

> *If I speak in tongues of men and of angels,*
> *but have not love, I am only a resounding*
> *gong or clanging cymbal.*
> *(1 Corinthians 13:1)*

One of the principles in the Army's leadership doctrine is this: "Know your soldiers and look out for their well-being." Effective leadership demands that leaders know their soldiers and demonstrate genuine caring for them.

One way to show concern is through words. Another way to show concern is through actions. And it's true — usually actions speak louder than words.

But there can still be a missing piece. Leaders can do and say all the "right" things and somehow fail to convey the message to soldiers that they really care.

The missing ingredient is what the Bible calls love. No, not the mushy, romantic kind of love most people associate with the word. Rather, it is a gut-level kind of caring that enables you to place high value on the lives and needs of your soldiers — at times, even above your own.

As a leader, don't just make noise. Show love to your soldiers — the kind of love God has shown you. ■

Encouragement in Spite of Difficulties

Now go out and encourage your men. I swear by the LORD that if you don't go out, not a man will be left with you by nightfall. This will be worse for you than all the calamities that have come upon you from your youth till now.
(2 Samuel 19:7)

This verse contains good counsel for any leader. David and his army had just fought a tough battle and won, but his son Absalom had been killed during the fighting. David was consumed with grief for his fallen son.

Joab, a veteran field general in King David's army, tells his leader the straight truth. He knows David is mourning the death of his son, Absalom. Nevertheless, the armies and people of Israel need David's leadership — NOW.

David heeds the advice. He puts his personal grief on the back burner and encourages his followers. He wins their hearts.

As difficult as it may be at times, leaders must continue to put the needs of others above their own.

Leaders, go encourage your people — NOW! ■

Feed My Sheep

Again Jesus said, "Simon son of John, do you truly love me?" He answered, "Yes, Lord, you know that I love you." Jesus said, "Take care of my sheep."
(John 21:16)

Can you imagine the scene? Peter is face-to-face with Jesus. The Lord asks, "Do you truly love me?" Then Jesus commands, "Feed my sheep."

The issue must have been important because Jesus asked the same question three times. Following each of Peter's responses, Jesus gave the same command: "Feed my sheep."

Do you see the connection? In large measure, our love for God can be seen in how we treat other people.

Do you love the Lord? If you say that you do, how are you treating His sheep — your soldiers, your spouse, your children, and other people?

Military leaders frequently use this saying: "I love my soldiers." The truth, however, is sometimes the soldiers don't believe the message. Why? Because, through their actions, leaders show they care more about themselves and their careers than about the people they lead. The troops know true caring when they see it.

Remember Jesus' command: "Feed my sheep." ■

Taking Action

Do to others as you would have them do to you.
(Luke 6:31)

Being a military leader in combat carries awesome responsibilities. The leader can make decisions and issue orders that require soldiers to put their lives on the line. Soldiers know this.

What do soldiers require of leaders in return? While the answers given by soldiers may differ in some ways, all soldiers need to know that leaders genuinely care about their welfare. Not just talk, but action. When you demonstrate caring through your actions, you can say "Follow me!" They will.

Jesus Christ knows all about soldiers and how to meet their needs. He gave us the Golden Rule. If you as a leader will consistently apply this principle in your treatment of soldiers, getting their loyalty and support will not be an issue.

One effective way to demonstrate the Golden Rule is to be with the troops in tough or dangerous situations. When you show your willingness to share hardships with them, it sends a powerful message to those you lead.

Not surprisingly, the Golden Rule works well in all kinds of situations. That's the way God intended it to be. ∎

Compassion Means Action

When Jesus landed and saw a large crowd, he had compassion on them and healed their sick.
(Matthew 14:14)

Compassion is an important trait for any leader. It sends a powerful message to soldiers that the leader genuinely cares about their welfare.

But the compassion expressed must be real. Troops see right through leaders who profess to have compassion but fail to deliver.

And how is compassion judged as being real or phony? The answer is simple — through action. Those to whom you express compassion in words wait to see if you follow with action.

Jesus provides us the best example of what compassion really means. The verse tells us Jesus had compassion toward the crowd and healed the sick.

It can be easy to rationalize and think that because we can't do all the miracles Jesus did, we don't need to try. Truthfully, when people come to you for help, most don't need a miracle as much as they need you simply to do the best you can. What seems like an ordinary action for you might seem like a miracle to them.

Jesus had compassion. His actions proved it. And so can yours. ■

Show Some Kindness

May the LORD repay you for what you have done.
May you be richly rewarded by the LORD,
the God of Israel, under whose wings you have
come to take refuge.
(Ruth 2:12).

The Book of Ruth contains a beautiful love story with many good lessons. In this verse, Boaz commends the young Moabite widow, Ruth, for her kindness shown toward her mother-in-law, Naomi.

It couldn't have been easy. Naomi's husband had died. But Ruth, a widow herself, overcame her own pain and encouraged her mother-in-law.

Military life serves up tough times. Everyone needs encouragement. When you reach out in kindness, you can be sure that you will have a positive impact on the lives of others. They will be encouraged.

Sometimes you may not be sure how to show kindness to someone who is hurting, especially those who may not have treated you very well. Trying to show kindness at times like this can be risky. Don't let that stop you.

And always remember this about showing kindness to others. God will richly reward you as well. So look around — most likely there is someone near you who could profit from a little kindness. ■

Love Gives Encouragement

Your love has given me great joy and encouragement, because you, brother, have refreshed the hearts of the saints.
(Philemon 7)

Military life can be tough. But everyone, even the most hardened warriors, are encouraged by acts of love.

A hardened veteran missionary himself, Paul expressed this fact in a letter. Philemon's love shown toward fellow believers brought joy and encouragement to Paul's heart.

Despite wartime conditions, U. S. troops in Iraq and Afghanistan have demonstrated love to children in both countries. Their actions have brought joy and encouragement not only to the kids, but also to millions of Americans back home.

Showing love doesn't require some special ability or high level of training. It boils down to a decision. You decide that you want to demonstrate love. It can be as simple as holding a door for someone or mowing the grass for a senior citizen. Or perhaps, you show God's love simply by listening patiently to another's person's problems.

Love never fails. Don't underestimate your ability to encourage many through your love shown to others.

Try it! ■

Adultery

Matthew 19:18

"Which ones?" the man inquired. Jesus replied, " 'Do not murder, do not commit adultery, do not steal, do not give false testimony.' "

Proverbs 5:3,4

For the lips of an adulteress drip honey, and her speech is smoother than oil; but in the end she is bitter as gall, sharp as a double-edged sword.

Anger

Proverbs 29:11

A fool gives full vent to his anger, but a wise man keeps himself under control.

Ephesians 4:26

"In your anger do not sin": Do not let the sun go down while you are still angry,

Anxiety

Philippians 4:6

Do not be anxious about anything, but in everything, by prayer and petition, with thanksgiving, present your requests to God.

1 Peter 5:6,7

Humble yourselves, therefore, under God's mighty hand, that he may lift you up in due time. Cast all your anxiety on him because he cares for you.

Backsliding

Ezekiel 37:23

They will no longer defile themselves with their idols and vile images or with any of their offenses, for I will save them from all their sinful backsliding, and I will cleanse them. They will be my people, and I will be their God.

Psalm 125:5

But those who turn to crooked ways the Lord will banish with the evildoers. Peace be upon Israel.

Bitterness

Ephesians 4:31

Get rid of all bitterness, rage and anger, brawling and slander, along with every form of malice.

James 3:14

But if you harbor bitter envy and selfish ambition in your hearts, do not boast about it or deny the truth.

Condemnation
John 3:18,19

Whoever believes in him is not condemned, but whoever does not believe stands condemned already because he has not believed in the name of God's one and only Son. This is the verdict: Light has come into the world, but men loved darkness instead of light because their deeds were evil.

Romans 8:1

Therefore, there is now no condemnation for those who are in Christ Jesus.

Confused
1 Corinthians 14:33

For God is not a God of disorder but of peace. As in all the congregations of the saints,

James 3:16

For where you have envy and selfish ambition, there you find disorder and every evil practice.

Contentment
Hebrews 13:5

Keep your lives free from the love of money and be content with what you have, because God has said, "Never will I leave you; never will I forsake you."

1 Timothy 6:6
But godliness with contentment is great gain.

Depressed

Psalm 121:1,2
I lift up my eyes to the hills— where does my help come from? My help comes from the Lord, the Maker of heaven and earth.

2 Corinthians 4:8,9
We are hard pressed on every side, but not crushed; perplexed, but not in despair; persecuted, but not abandoned; struck down, but not destroyed.

Despairing

Psalm 42:11
Why are you downcast, O my soul? Why so disturbed within me? Put your hope in God, for I will yet praise him, my Savior and my God.

1 Peter 5:7
Cast all your anxiety on him because he cares for you.

Disobedience

2 Corinthians 10:6
And we will be ready to punish every act of disobedience, once your obedience is complete.

James 1:14,5

But each one is tempted when, by his own evil desire, he is dragged away and enticed. Then, after desire has conceived, it gives birth to sin; and sin, when it is full–grown, gives birth to death.

Divorce

Malachi 2:16

"I hate divorce," says the Lord God of Israel, "and I hate a man's covering himself with violence as well as with his garment," says the Lord Almighty. So guard yourself in your spirit, and do not break faith.

Mark 10:8,9

And the two will become one flesh.' So they are no longer two, but one. Therefore what God has joined together, let man not separate."

Doubting

Matthew 21:21

Jesus replied, "I tell you the truth, if you have faith and do not doubt, not only can you do what was done to the fig tree, but also you can say to this mountain, 'Go, throw yourself into the sea,' and it will be done.

James 1:6,7

But when he asks, he must believe and not doubt, because he who doubts is like a wave of the sea, blown and tossed by the wind. That man should not think he will receive anything from the Lord.

Endurance

Matthew 10:22

All men will hate you because of me, but he who stands firm to the end will be saved.

2 Timothy 2:3

Endure hardship with us like a good soldier of Christ Jesus.

Enemies

Luke 6:27,28

"But I tell you who hear me: Love your enemies, do good to those who hate you, bless those who curse you, pray for those who mistreat you.

Luke 6:35

But love your enemies, do good to them, and lend to them without expecting to get anything back. Then your reward will be great, and you will be sons of the Most High, because he is kind to the ungrateful and wicked.

Romans 12:14

Bless those who persecute you; bless and do not curse.

Excuses

John 15:22

If I had not come and spoken to them, they would not
be guilty of sin. Now, however, they have no excuse for
their sin.

Romans 1:20

For since the creation of the world God's invisible
qualities—his eternal power and divine nature—have
been clearly seen, being understood from what has
been made, so that men are without excuse.

Faith

John 6:29

Jesus answered, "The work of God is this: to believe in
the one he has sent."

Hebrews 11:1

Now faith is being sure of what we hope for and
certain of what we do not see.

Romans 10:9,10

That if you confess with your mouth, "Jesus is Lord,"
and believe in your heart that God raised him from the
dead, you will be saved. For it is with your heart that
you believe and are justified, and it is with your mouth
that you confess and are saved.

Fear

Isaiah 41:10

So do not fear, for I am with you; do not be dismayed, for I am your God. I will strengthen you and help you; I will uphold you with my righteous right hand.

2 Timothy 1:7

For God did not give us a spirit of timidity, but a spirit of power, of love and of self-discipline.

Fear of God

Proverbs 1:7

The fear of the Lord is the beginning of knowledge, but fools despise wisdom and discipline.

Proverbs 19:23

The fear of the Lord leads to life: Then one rests content, untouched by trouble.

Fear of Man

Proverbs 29:25

Fear of man will prove to be a snare, but whoever trusts in the Lord is kept safe.

Luke 12:4,5

"I tell you, my friends, do not be afraid of those who kill the body and after that can do no more. But I will show you whom you should fear: Fear him who, after the killing of the body, has power to throw you into hell. Yes, I tell you, fear him.

Forgiveness
Matthew 18:21,22

Then Peter came to Jesus and asked, "Lord, how many times shall I forgive my brother when he sins against me? Up to seven times?" Jesus answered, "I tell you, not seven times, but seventy-seven times."

Ephesians 4:32

Be kind and compassionate to one another, forgiving each other, just as in Christ God forgave you.

Fruitfulness
John 12:24

I tell you the truth, unless a kernel of wheat falls to the ground and dies, it remains only a single seed. But if it dies, it produces many seeds.

John 15:5

"I am the vine; you are the branches. If a man remains in me and I in him, he will bear much fruit; apart from me you can do nothing."

God's Will

2 Peter 3:9

The Lord is not slow in keeping his promise, as some understand slowness. He is patient with you, not wanting anyone to perish, but everyone to come to repentance.

1 Thessalonians 4:3–5

It is God's will that you should be sanctified: that you should avoid sexual immorality; that each of you should learn to control his own body in a way that is holy and honorable, not in passionate lust like the heathen, who do not know God.

1 Thessalonians 5:18

Give thanks in all circumstances, for this is God's will for you in Christ Jesus.

1 Peter 2:15

For it is God's will that by doing good you should silence the ignorant talk of foolish men.

Godliness

1 Timothy 6:11

But you, man of God, flee from all this, and pursue righteousness, godliness, faith, love, endurance and gentleness.

1 Timothy 6:6

But godliness with contentment is great gain.

Grace

1 Corinthians 12:9

But he said to me, "My grace is sufficient for you, for my power is made perfect in weakness." Therefore I will boast all the more gladly about my weaknesses, so that Christ's power may rest on me.

Romans 5:15

But the gift is not like the trespass. For if the many died by the trespass of the one man, how much more did God's grace and the gift that came by the grace of the one man, Jesus Christ, overflow to the many!

Greed

Luke 12:15

Then he said to them, "Watch out! Be on your guard against all kinds of greed; a man's life does not consist in the abundance of his possessions."

Colossians 3:5

Put to death, therefore, whatever belongs to your earthly nature: sexual immorality, impurity, lust, evil desires and greed, which is idolatry.

Grief

John 16:20

I tell you the truth, you will weep and mourn while the world rejoices. You will grieve, but your grief will turn to joy.

1 Peter 1:6

In this you greatly rejoice, though now for a little while you may have had to suffer grief in all kinds of trials.

Guidance

Psalm 73:24

You guide me with your counsel, and afterward you will take me into glory.

John 16:13

But when he, the Spirit of truth, comes, he will guide you into all truth. He will not speak on his own; he will speak only what he hears, and he will tell you what is yet to come.

Honor

Romans 12:10

Be devoted to one another in brotherly love. Honor one another above yourselves.

1 Corinthians 6:20

You were bought at a price. Therefore honor God with your body.

Ephesians 6:2

"Honor your father and mother" — which is the first commandment with a promise.

Proverbs 20:3

It is to a man's honor to avoid strife, but every fool is quick to quarrel.

Hope

Romans 8:24

For in this hope we were saved. But hope that is seen is no hope at all. Who hopes for what he already has?

1 Peter 1:3

Praise be to the God and Father of our Lord Jesus Christ! In his great mercy he has given us new birth into a living hope through the resurrection of Jesus Christ from the dead.

Humility

Philippians 2:3

Do nothing out of selfish ambition or vain conceit, but in humility consider others better than yourselves.

Colossians 3:12

Therefore, as God's chosen people, holy and dearly loved, clothe yourselves with compassion, kindness, humility, gentleness and patience.

James 3:13

Who is wise and understanding among you? Let him show it by his good life, by deeds done in the humility that comes from wisdom.

Integrity

Proverbs 10:9

The man of integrity walks securely, but he who takes crooked paths will be found out.

Proverbs 29:11

A fool gives full vent to his anger, but a wise man keeps himself under control.

Joy

John 15:11

I have told you this so that my joy may be in you and that your joy may be complete.

John 16:20

I tell you the truth, you will weep and mourn while the world rejoices. You will grieve, but your grief will turn to joy.

James 1:2

Consider it pure joy, my brothers, whenever you face trials of many kinds.

Justice

Matthew 23:23

"Woe to you, teachers of the law and Pharisees, you hypocrites! You give a tenth of your spices — mint, dill and cummin. But you have neglected the more important matters of the law — justice, mercy and faithfulness. You should have practiced the latter, without neglecting the former."

Luke 18:7

And will not God bring about justice for his chosen ones, who cry out to him day and night? Will he keep putting them off?

Revelation 19:11

I saw heaven standing open and there before me was a white horse, whose rider is called Faithful and True. With justice he judges and makes war.

Kindness

Acts 14:17

Yet he has not left himself without testimony: He has shown kindness by giving you rain from heaven and crops in their seasons; he provides you with plenty of food and fills your hearts with joy.

Galatians 5:22,23
But the fruit of the Spirit is love, joy, peace, patience, kindness, goodness, faithfulness, gentleness and self-control. Against such things there is no law.

Life

Matthew 10:39
Whoever finds his life will lose it, and whoever loses his life for my sake will find it.

Matthew 19:39
And everyone who has left houses or brothers or sisters or father or mother or children or fields for my sake will receive a hundred times as much and will inherit eternal life.

John 3:16
For God so loved the world that he gave his one and only Son, that whoever believes in him shall not perish but have eternal life.

1 John 5:12
He who has the Son has life; he who does not have the Son of God does not have life.

Loneliness

Psalm 68:6

God sets the lonely in families, he leads forth the prisoners with singing; but the rebellious live in a sun-scorched land.

2 Timothy 4:16,17

At my first defense, no one came to my support, but everyone deserted me. May it not be held against them. But the Lord stood at my side and gave me strength, so that through me the message might be fully proclaimed and all the Gentiles might hear it. And I was delivered from the lion's mouth.

Love

1 Peter 4:8

Above all, love each other deeply, because love covers over a multitude of sins.

1 John 5:3

This is love for God: to obey his commands. And his commands are not burdensome.

James 2:8

If you really keep the royal law found in Scripture, "Love your neighbor as yourself," you are doing right.

Lust

Proverbs 6:25

Do not lust in your heart after her beauty or let her captivate you with her eyes.

Colossians 3:5

Put to death, therefore, whatever belongs to your earthly nature: sexual immorality, impurity, lust, evil desires and greed, which is idolatry.

1 John 2:16

For everything in the world — the cravings of sinful man, the lust of his eyes and the boasting of what he has and does — comes not from the Father but from the world.

Money

Matthew 6:24

No one can serve two masters. Either he will hate the one and love the other, or he will be devoted to the one and despise the other. You cannot serve both God and Money.

1 Timothy 6:10

For the love of money is a root of all kinds of evil. Some people, eager for money, have wandered from the faith and pierced themselves with many griefs.

Obedience

Romans 1:5

Through him and for his name's sake, we received grace and apostleship to call people from among all the Gentiles to the obedience that comes from faith.

2 John 6

And this is love: that we walk in obedience to his commands. As you have heard from the beginning, his command is that you walk in love.

Overwhelmed

Psalm 38:4

My guilt has overwhelmed me like a burden too heavy to bear.

Matthew 26:38

Then he said to them, "My soul is overwhelmed with sorrow to the point of death. Stay here and keep watch with me."

Patience

Proverbs 19:11

A man's wisdom gives him patience; it is to his glory to overlook an offense.

Colossians 1:11

Being strengthened with all power according to his glorious might so that you may have great endurance and patience.

Galatians 5:22,23

But the fruit of the Spirit is love, joy, peace, patience, kindness, goodness, faithfulness, gentleness and self-control. Against such things there is no law.

Perseverance

Hebrews 10:36

You need to persevere so that when you have done the will of God, you will receive what he has promised.

James 1:12

Blessed is the man who perseveres under trial, because when he has stood the test, he will receive the crown of life that God has promised to those who love him.

Plans

Psalm 33:11

But the plans of the Lord stand firm forever, the purposes of his heart through all generations.

Proverbs 15:22

Plans fail for lack of counsel, but with many advisers they succeed.

Proverbs 16:3

Commit to the Lord whatever you do, and your plans will succeed.

Jeremiah 29:11

"For I know the plans I have for you," declares the Lord, "plans to prosper you and not to harm you, plans to give you hope and a future."

Praise

Hebrews 13:15

Through Jesus, therefore, let us continually offer to God a sacrifice of praise—the fruit of lips that confess his name.

Psalm 33:1

Sing joyfully to the Lord, you righteous; it is fitting for the upright to praise him.

John 12:43

They loved praise from men more than praise from God.

Prayer

Psalm 6:9

The Lord has heard my cry for mercy; the Lord accepts my prayer.

1 Peter 3:12

For the eyes of the Lord are on the righteous and his ears are attentive to their prayer, but the face of the Lord is against those who do evil.

Pride

Proverbs 8:13

To fear the Lord is to hate evil; I hate pride and arrogance, evil behavior and perverse speech.

Proverbs 16:18

Pride goes before destruction, a haughty spirit before a fall.

Rest

Jeremiah 6:16

This is what the Lord says: "Stand at the crossroads and look; ask for the ancient paths, ask where the good way is, and walk in it, and you will find rest for your souls. But you said, 'We will not walk in it.'"

Matthew 11:28

"Come to me, all you who are weary and burdened, and I will give you rest."

Mark 6:31

Then, because so many people were coming and going that they did not even have a chance to eat, he said to them, "Come with me by yourselves to a quiet place and get some rest."

Revenge

Leviticus 19:18

"'Do not seek revenge or bear a grudge against one of your people, but love your neighbor as yourself. I am the Lord."

Romans 12:19

Do not take revenge, my friends, but leave room for God's wrath, for it is written: "It is mine to avenge; I will repay," says the Lord.

Righteousness

Matthew 5:6

Blessed are those who hunger and thirst for righteousness, for they will be filled.

Romans 3:21,22

But now a righteousness from God, apart from law, has been made known, to which the Law and the Prophets testify. This righteousness from God comes through faith in Jesus Christ to all who believe.

2 Corinthians 5:21

God made him who had no sin to be sin for us, so that in him we might become the righteousness of God.

Salvation

John 3:16

For God so loved the world that he gave his one and only Son, that whoever believes in him shall not perish but have eternal life.

Ephesians 2:8–10

For it is by grace you have been saved, through faith — and this not from yourselves, it is the gift of God — not by works, so that no one can boast. For we are God's workmanship, created in Christ Jesus to do good works, which God prepared in advance for us to do.

Self-control

1 Peter 4:7

The end of all things is near. Therefore be clear minded and self-controlled so that you can pray.

Titus 2:12

It teaches us to say "No" to ungodliness and worldly passions, and to live self–controlled, upright and godly lives in this present age.

Speech Strength

Psalm 28:7

The Lord is my strength and my shield; my heart trusts in him, and I am helped. My heart leaps for joy and I will give thanks to him in song.

1 Corinthians 1:25

For the foolishness of God is wiser than man's wisdom, and the weakness of God is stronger than man's strength.

Submission

Romans 13:1

Everyone must submit himself to the governing authorities, for there is no authority except that which God has established. The authorities that exist have been established by God.

Ephesians 5:21

Submit to one another out of reverence for Christ.

Hebrews 12:9

Moreover, we have all had human fathers who disciplined us and we respected them for it. How much more should we submit to the Father of our spirits and live!

Hebrews 13:17

Obey your leaders and submit to their authority. They keep watch over you as men who must give an account. Obey them so that their work will be a joy, not a burden, for that would be of no advantage to you.

Suffering

Romans 8:17,18

Now if we are children, then we are heirs—heirs of God and co-heirs with Christ, if indeed we share in his sufferings in order that we may also share in his glory. I consider that our present sufferings are not worth comparing with the glory that will be revealed in us.

Swearing

Colossians 3:8

But now you must rid yourselves of all such things as these: anger, rage, malice, slander, and filthy language from your lips.

Temptation

Matthew 6:13

"And lead us not into temptation, but deliver us from the evil one."

1 Corinthians 10:13

No temptation has seized you except what is common to man. And God is faithful; he will not let you be tempted beyond what you can bear. But when you are tempted, he will also provide a way out so that you can stand up under it.

James 1:13,14

When tempted, no one should say, "God is tempting me." For God cannot be tempted by evil, nor does he tempt anyone; but each one is tempted when, by his own evil desire, he is dragged away and enticed.

Thankfulness

Psalm 100:4

Enter his gates with thanksgiving and his courts with praise; give thanks to him and praise his name.

Philippians 4:6

Do not be anxious about anything, but in everything, by prayer and petition, with thanksgiving, present your requests to God.

Trouble

John 16:33

I have told you these things, so that in me you may have peace. In this world you will have trouble. But take heart! I have overcome the world.

Romans 8:35,37

Who shall separate us from the love of Christ? Shall trouble or hardship or persecution or famine or nakedness or danger or sword? . . . No, in all these things we are more than conquerors through him who loved us.

Trust

Proverbs 3:5,6

Trust in the Lord with all your heart and lean not on your own understanding; in all your ways acknowledge him, and he will make your paths straight.

John 14:1

Do not let your hearts be troubled. Trust in God; trust also in me.

Truth

John 8:32

Then you will know the truth, and the truth will set you free.

2 Timothy 2:15

Do your best to present yourself to God as one approved, a workman who does not need to be ashamed and who correctly handles the word of truth.

Victory

Psalm 60:12

With God we will gain the victory, and he will trample down our enemies.

1 Corinthians 15:57

But thanks be to God! He gives us the victory through our Lord Jesus Christ.

Weariness

Matthew 11:28

"Come to me, all you who are weary and burdened, and I will give you rest."

Galatians 6:9

Let us not become weary in doing good, for at the proper time we will reap a harvest if we do not give up.

Words

Proverbs 25:11

A word aptly spoken is like apples of gold in settings of silver.

Proverbs 30:5

Every word of God is flawless; he is a shield to those who take refuge in him.

Work

Exodus 23:12

"Six days do your work, but on the seventh day do not work, so that your ox and your donkey may rest and the slave born in your household, and the alien as well, may be refreshed."

Colossians 3:23

Whatever you do, work at it with all your heart, as working for the Lord, not for men,

Worship

Psalm 95:6

Come, let us bow down in worship, let us kneel before the Lord our Maker;

Romans 12:1

Therefore, I urge you, brothers, in view of God's mercy, to offer your bodies as living sacrifices, holy and pleasing to God—this is your spiritual act of worship.

Chaplain (COL)
Scott McChrystal, USA (Ret)

Chaplain (Colonel) Scott McChrystal was commissioned in 1970 as a 2Lt in the infantry. He served 31 years on active duty, 10 as an infantry officer and the remainder as an Army chaplain. His line officer experience included a tour in Vietnam as an Infantry Platoon Leader and three assignments with the 82nd Airborne Division at Fort Bragg, North Carolina. As an Army chaplain, he had multiple tours at home and abroad. His final assignment was at the senior chaplain at the United States Military Academy at West Point, New York. He retired from active duty in 2005.

His decorations and awards include the Distinguished Service Award, the Bronze Star, the Combat Infantryman's Badge, the Master Parachutist Badge, and the Army Ranger Tab.

Chaplain McChrystal presently serves as the Military/VA Representative and Endorser within the Chaplaincy Department for the General Council of the Assemblies of God. Chaplain McChrystal and his wife, Judy, live in Springfield, Missouri, and have four children: Beth, 42; Mary, 33, Robert, 29; and Joshua, 22. ■

On the left, 1Lt Scott McChrystal and his infantry platoon wait for helicopters that will insert them on a search and destroy mission to the west of Danang, South Vietnam, 1971. Above, Chaplain McChrystal prepares to deliver a public prayer at the United States Military Academy at West Point, New York, 2003.

A Message from Scott

I hope you've been encouraged and strengthened as you've read this book. *Daily Strength for the Battle: Training for Spiritual Excellence*, as its name implies, is designed to get you started on a powerful journey of transformation. The volumes to follow will offer you additional resources for spiritual growth.

The second volume of *Daily Strength for the Battle*, *Strengthening Your Spiritual Foundation*, takes the view that many skilled and capable people experience frustration in their Christian walk. This can be due to a poor foundation in the basics of Christian growth. But let's admit it, the grind of daily life in today's world can render even established Christians temporarily ineffective. I'm convinced the right spiritual training will produce the growth you're seeking.

In volume 2 you will concentrate on the following areas: Knowing God's Word, Growing through Prayer, Learning Submission, Serving Others, Knowing Your Enemy, Maturing through Relationships, and Controlling Your Thought Life.

Additional copies of this volume,
as well as future volumes, are available at
Our Web site: www.dailystrengthforthebattle.com
By e-mail: contact@dailystrengthforthebattle.com
By mail: Warrior Spirit Publications
P.O. Box 8125, Springfield, MO 65801

Notes

Notes

Notes